THE WRITING AND SELLING OF NON-FICTION

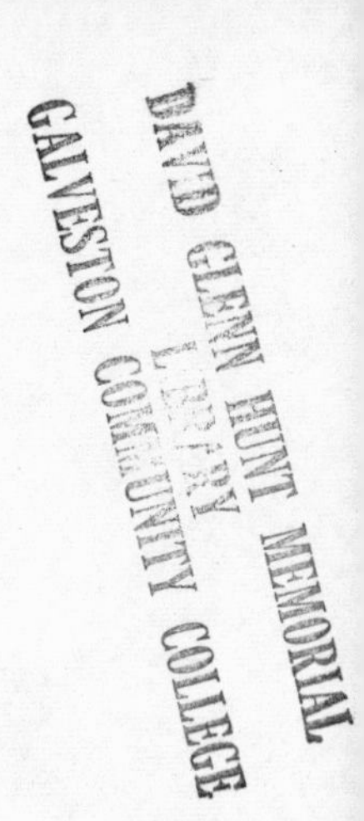

Also by Paul R. Reynolds

THE WRITER AND HIS MARKETS

THE WRITING TRADE

TO

CHARLES W. FERGUSON

THE EXPERT EDITOR

THE CHARMING SPEAKER

THE BRILLIANT WRITER

INTRODUCTION

For a week during the summers of 1961 and 1962 I conducted a seminar at the University of Georgia's Center for Continuing Education. My subject was the writing and selling of non-fiction. This book is an outgrowth of these lectures.

If a person wants to be a painter, musician, or novelist, the first question asked is whether the person possesses the requisite talent. To a person wanting to write non-fiction the question is not germane. No special talent is necessary for the writing of non-fiction. In this respect the occupation is similar to medicine or law. Competence in these professions requires reasonable intelligence and the willingness to undertake a long learning process, a long apprenticeship. It is the same with the non-fiction writer, although the apprenticeship is shorter. Anyone with reasonable intelligence who will undergo the learning process can write publishable non-fiction. How successful a writer will be is unpredictable. The same can be said of any other occupation.

Because the non-fiction writer does not have to acquire a large mass of information about his profession, because everyone writes letters and can put words together, the learning process necessary to master non-fiction writing is often ignored. But the learning process is there and is essential. It requires many months of concentrated effort. The techniques and skills can be outlined in a book. They can be absorbed only in connection with the process of writing.

The painter or musician receives pleasure and satisfaction from his skill even if there is no financial remuneration. The writer is different. He writes to be read, and without publication has nothing. Publication usually means selling the manuscript. Hence this book discusses the problems connected with publication and with financial rewards.

Discouragement is the bane of the writer. In nine out of ten cases his discouragement has no basis in reason. The author fails to sell because he has tried to obtain publication before he has learned his trade. He is trying to run before he has learned to walk. This book is an attempt to take the reader through the steps of the learning process. If it dispels some of the discouragement so inherent in the world of the written word, it will have served its purpose.

Paul R. Reynolds
CHAPPAQUA, NEW YORK

THE WRITING AND SELLING OF NON-FICTION

PART I

1

DEVELOPING THE THEME-IDEA

This chapter and the two following will discuss writing the popular article. The magazine article is an entity in itself, a non-fiction piece with a beginning, a middle, and an end. It should leave the reader with a theory or conviction about a related set of facts, or with an emotional attitude towards a related set of facts, or with a belief in the truth or falsehood of one or more statements or theories based upon a set of related facts.

The techniques necessary to produce a successful magazine article are, with variations, the techniques useful for all non-fiction writing. A successful magazine writer can learn with little trouble to handle most forms of non-fiction writing.

Writers of non-fiction can be divided into categories. There are people making their first attempt to write; there are people who have completed manuscripts which they are unable to get published; there are people who have occasionally published but who have not learned to write salable pieces with consistency. This book will call such individuals "writers-in-training." Writers who sell a number of articles each year so as to materially increase their income will be called professionals. There is no clear distinction between writers-in-training and professionals. It is a matter of degree. Every professional started writing unpublishable manuscripts, and went through a writer-in-training period. The professional, no matter how successful, retains one quality in common with the writer-in-training; the professional is still learning.

The first step in preparing an article, for both the writer-in-training and the professional, is to select the subject matter. Authors do not have trouble selecting subject matter. A general subject such as unemployment, or automobile accidents, or African wild animals is possible. A more specific subject may be chosen. The animals seen through a microscope in a drop of water may be possible subjects for one or more articles. A woman who has done a great deal of gardening, read many books on trees and flowers, visited and examined with care many gardens and landscapes, probably starts her writing in the field of flowers, shrubs, and trees. Her knowledge and interest has determined her subject area, and she will find little difficulty in selecting specific subject matter.

Everyone knows what subject matter is. In most cases a writer only uses part of a subject matter. An article dealing with automobile racing does not cover all aspects of automobile racing. The article will deal with a particular driver, or a particular race track, or a particular type of racing car, etc. If automobile racing is the general subject matter, a particular race track is a segment of the subject matter. However, a segment of a subject matter is not in itself an idea for an article. The particular race track, the description of it, the history of it, is not an idea for an article. But a race track which has the fewest accidents, or the most accidents, or the track where the world's speed record has been broken, or the largest or longest track in the world, or the most colorful track may become an idea for an article. In other words, there must be a theme, a point of view towards the facts, often an emotional feeling. An idea with a theme for a non-fiction piece may be defined as a point of view, often with emotional overtones, towards a segment of a subject matter. This book will call such a point of view the "theme-idea."

The theme-idea is all important. It is the compass, the director, and the determiner of the material used in the piece.

The theme-idea is the mental control which will guide the author in preparing the structural design of his piece. No one can write an article (or, for that matter, a book) without a theme-idea. Here is a list of subject matters and theme-ideas picked at random from magazine articles.

SUBJECT MATTERS	THEME-IDEAS
Garbage disposal	The blight of the Athens garbage dump.
Trees	Trees live until disease kills them. They do not die of old age.
Fish	A study and discussion of the pain a hooked fish suffers.
Nuclear fallout	Nuclear fallout—the case against shelters.
Flirting	How flirting adds an exuberance and charm to friendships between men and women.
Lady astronauts	A description of the rigorous training a lady astronaut undergoes.
Preparing a meal	The forty-nine steps necessary to prepare a meal.
Barkeepers	How the best barkeepers learn their trade.

The above list is completely haphazard and can be expanded indefinitely. Here are some examples in more detail:

In the April 25, 1961 issue of *Look* magazine is an article entitled "Atlanta: 1864—A Man's Battle Fought by Boys." A battle of the Civil War is the subject matter. The

Battle of Atlanta is a particular segment of the subject matter. The theme-idea in this case is expressed in the title.

In *The Saturday Evening Post* of April 8, 1961, is an article entitled "New York's New Queen of Fashion." Here again the title is a theme-idea for an article. Facts about Pauline Trigère is the subject matter. Facts about her as a fashion designer is the segment of the subject matter. What gives the article a theme-idea is the treatment of Pauline Trigère as the *Queen* of New York's fashion.

In the March 1961 issue of the *Reader's Digest* is an article entitled "A Seat Belt Could Save Your Life." The theme-idea of the article is: use automobile seat belts because your life in the car can be safer. Seat belts is the subject matter. Automobile seat belts is the segment of the subject matter. How automobile seat belts can save your life produces a theme-idea.

Authors often assume that a segment of a subject matter is a theme-idea. A description of the Battle of Atlanta, a short profile of Pauline Trigère, a description of how the auto seat belt works, none of these are in themselves theme-ideas. They are just subject matter or parts of subject matter and will be referred to in this book as the nuclei of ideas.

As a rule a theme-idea does not come to an author full-blown. Theme-ideas do not spontaneously appear. One cannot pick up a theme-idea the way one can pick up a pencil from a table. However, the nucleus of an idea, the spark from which a good theme-idea may be ultimately developed, can be found.

Writers get the nucleus of an idea from some sentence in a magazine piece, or from something in a book, or from a sentence heard in casual conversation, or from some unusual fact they have observed. Looking in one direction an author may find the nucleus of an idea in another. From the nucleus the writer develops the theme-idea. Perhaps the writer thinks of alcohol and drinking as a possible subject matter for an article. Then perhaps he gets the nucleus of an idea, a piece on barmaids. He inquires of a barkeeper in New York City as to whether there are any barmaids in the area. The barkeeper perhaps says: "Not that I know of, but when I was in school studying to be a barkeeper, there was one woman student." The writer jumps at the discovery that barkeepers go to school to learn to be proficient in their jobs, finds that there are three schools for barkeepers in New York City, and develops a theme-idea for an article on the training of a barkeeper.

Perhaps an author wants to write about the problems of feeding the world with its ever increasing population. He has an area of interest. Perhaps he thinks of the six sevenths of the world's surface that is covered with water, and finally comes up with plankton, a food which supports fish and may itself, possibly, be a food for human beings. Now he has a subject matter obtained perhaps by chance or perhaps through purposeful research. The author discovers that plankton feeds little fish at the bottom of the sea, that little fish feed big fish, and that men catch and eat big fish. The author has the nucleus of an idea with regard to the feeding of the world. Perhaps in his reading he discovers an instrument, the aqua-therm, which will bring plankton up to the surface of the sea where it can be harvested. Now he has a theme-idea for an article: the aqua-therm, how it can feed the starving.

Here is a third example. An author thinks of garbage as a subject matter. Let us suppose that there is a town of Athens, Idaho, which has a large open public garbage dump. A garbage dump is a segment of a subject matter, and the Athens garbage dump is a particular segment and the nucleus of a theme-idea. Let us suppose that this garbage dump is an eyesore, lowers property values to a slum-area level, and above all, is a health menace. Now the author has "The Blight of the Athens Garbage Dump" as a theme-idea. He has a point of view and an emotional approach towards a particular segment of a subject matter, towards a particular garbage dump.

Most theme-ideas are developed in the course of preliminary research. A successful writer is engaged in research from the time of selection of the subject matter until his piece is completed. The amateur in his first writing attempt is apt to ignore research and just write off the top of his head. He tends to concentrate on his own thoughts about some subject. His written piece is often akin to a personal letter, except that he wants to sell what he has composed for strangers to read, rather than give what he has composed for a friend to read. What the amateur often does is similar to what the average high school student does when he writes a theme for English composition. He tends to write a description of some autobiographical incident. Because the author ignores research he finds it difficult to obtain a theme-idea. Professional writers immerse themselves in research. The writer-in-training should do likewise. The first purpose of research is to find one or more nuclei of ideas. The second purpose of research is to stimulate the imagination further and help develop the nucleus of an idea into a theme-idea.

A theme-idea can be expressed in one, or possibly two, sentences. Because the theme-idea has been developed from research, from the nucleus of an idea, because it has been developed in one's conscious and unconscious mind, it often has more meaning to the author than is apparent, more meaning than seems to appear in its sentence or two of description.

Research may be divided into two categories, *live* and *library*. Live research is obtained from interviewing people, from conversation, and from examining physical objects. Library research is reading about the subject, or about a segment of it. The reading is of books, magazines, newspapers, and occasionally of original manuscripts or letters.

Every theme-idea requires both live and library research

before a successful article can be developed. The theme-idea for an article on the training of barkeepers was obtained through live research, but before the article is finished there should be some reading, perhaps the curriculum of the students studying to be barkeepers if nothing else. The plankton idea was obtained solely through library research, but some live research should ultimately be done. It would be desirable for the writer to look at plankton, eat it, try cooking it in various ways, etc. Also, how about interviewing a diver who had seen the plant at the bottom of the ocean? Anyone writing about garbage and garbage disposal would do well to read articles on the subject. Curiously enough, there have been many. A purely scholarly subject such as Egyptian mummies would obviously require chiefly library research, but, if possible, some live research should be done. Going to Egypt and looking at mummies would probably not be practical; but one bit of live research would be helpful. The writer should interview some Egyptologist or expert on the subject. Suppose one was writing an article on the heroism of certain Cuban exiles who tried to invade Cuba and overthrow Castro. The article would be primarily live research, interviewing survivors who took part in the invasion, examining their boats, equipment etc. But library research would also play a part. The weather, the tides, the rocks should be studied in the library. Newspaper accounts should be read.

There are many ramifications to library research. Let us refer to the plankton theme-idea. The writer should examine the *Reader's Guide to Periodical Literature,* which most libraries have. There he discovers that the August 1955 issue of *Nature Magazine,* and the February 25, 1956 issue of *Science News Letter* each contains an article on the subject matter. Here is library research. Both of these articles the writer, whether professional or writer-in-training, should read. Perhaps the author has never heard of *Science News*

Letter. He must be a detective, find out, and ultimately obtain a copy.

This process of selecting one's subject matter, getting the nucleus of an idea, and then through research obtaining a theme-idea seems easy and is easy. Anyone can get theme-ideas. The problem is to get good ones. How does an author tell whether a theme-idea is a good one or not? A man learns how to tie his necktie. The operation becomes so instinctive that he would find it difficult to describe the exact movements of each finger. Likewise, a professional writer cannot tell how he develops and evaluates a theme-idea. The entire process becomes instinctive. The writer-in-training has to learn step by step.

As soon as a writer has a theme-idea which he thinks he might want to use, he should investigate to what extent the same theme-idea or related ones have previously been published. If the author's theme-idea has been developed pretty exactly in a published piece, the writer will probably decide to drop this particular project. If the theme-idea has been partially used, or if a variation of it has been used, then the author should say to himself: "Can I produce a better article on the subject matter? Can I obtain new material which the previous writer did not have or use? Have I a more interesting point of view, a somewhat different, more interesting theme-idea?"

An author writing a magazine article thinks of other magazine articles for his research, but he should also look in the library for books on the subject. Perhaps there are no books directly applicable, but there may be books with chapters or references to his segment of subject matter and to his theme-idea. If the theme-idea has never been partially used or touched upon, the author probably has a poor theme-idea; at least this should be considered a danger signal. It is doubtful if any author is so original and so imaginative that he has developed a really good theme-idea which no other writer has previously thought of even in a partial or fragmentary form.

Early in his research an author should ask himself the following questions about his theme-idea:

1. Are there sufficient facts which the author can obtain for an interesting piece?

For example, what can an author say about plankton? The difficulty of obtaining or harvesting it, the possibility of planting it, the amount in existence, what it looks like, ways of cooking it? Maybe there are enough facts related to the theme-idea to justify a good piece, or maybe not. If a theme-idea can be fully developed in one or two paragraphs, there is no possibility of a full-length article. Readers are not interested in repetition or padding. The only possibility is a half-page magazine filler. Suppose a writer wants to do a piece on why a passenger plane crashed. Perhaps the theme-idea is that carelessness caused forty-two deaths. If the cause of the accident was human failure, if a mechanic failed to do one simple thing he should have done, there is probably no article on the theme-idea of why the plane crashed. The reason can be explained in a paragraph or two. However, there may well be a piece in a description of the crash, the courage of the stewardess, etc. This would call for a different theme-idea.

2. Is the theme-idea one that would interest a substantial number of people?

Suppose the author has a theme-idea "How To Hitchhike Successfully." An article told from the point of view of hitchhikers would presumably interest hitchhikers, but how many hitchhikers are there? And how many hitchhikers are avid readers? However, an article on the motorist picking up hitchhikers, perhaps with the theme-idea "Hitchhikers Can Rob or Murder You," presumably has a broad base of interest. Everyone drives a car and has picked up or refused to pick up hitchhikers. If a theme-idea might interest anyone or might interest anyone in a particular occupation or area, it is a possibility.

For example an article with a theme-idea about cancer ostensibly would appeal to anyone. Every person knows of someone who has died of cancer. An article with a theme-idea around some obscure disease would have little interest to the general public; it might be so written as to be very interesting to doctors. In other words, cancer may be written up for everyone or just for doctors; an obscure disease, probably just for doctors.

3. Is the theme-idea important or can it be made to seem important to the reader?

Leaving out of consideration the humorous article, people rarely want to read about trivia. There are hundreds, maybe thousands of buttons of different shapes and sizes. Perhaps there could be an article on the theme-idea of the desirability of having only fifty-seven varieties of buttons. But is the subject important enough? Is an article on "The Blight of the Athens Garbage Dump" important enough? The answer is quite likely in the negative, but perhaps the article can be made to seem important. If the dump is a real health menace to the people of Athens, Idaho, the subject becomes important to them, and might be suitable to a newspaper circulating in the town. If the dump is little or no menace to health, if it is nothing but an eyesore and nuisance, the theme-idea, and hence the article, will be unimportant.

4. Does the writer know of a market where the theme-idea would seem to be suitable?

In a later chapter marketing will be discussed, but unless the theme-idea would seem to fit some magazine or newspaper that the author thinks he can write for, the theme-idea should be rejected. For example, a theme-idea based on an obscure bit of European history might be difficult to find a medium for, but a theme-idea based on an obscure bit of American history might be suitable for *American Heritage*.

There are questions the author should ask himself about special types of articles. If an author has a theme-idea for an informative article, has he reason to believe that people want to know the facts or does the author think they ought to know them? If the latter, the theme-idea probably is not very good. An article on how to obtain an automobile seat strap and install it in the seat and use it may be something everyone should know about, but query whether people want to know about it. If the theme-idea is for an emotional piece, the questions differ. Will the theme-idea ring a bell with all of us? Will it appeal and move a clerk in a hardware store in Killicot, Iowa? A moving piece on "Automobile Straps as Life Savers" obviously may appeal to anyone. An article on a humane way to hunt and kill deer may appeal to all animal lovers, but it may not have the impact that a dog or cat piece may have; too few people hunt deer. Will the piece seem trite? If the article is going to advocate the obvious, such as obeying traffic rules and not speeding, the piece probably will seem trite regardless of how much such injunctions may be needed. If the theme-idea has been written up a great deal, it may seem trite unless the author has a very original and ingenious method of presentation.

All of the above questions deal with matters of degree, which the author has to judge for himself. The instructor cannot be dogmatic. He can only suggest methods of training. One method which may help an author evaluate his theme-idea is to study a large number of published articles, list the theme-ideas of each, and then try to judge to what extent the author's theme-idea seems to fulfill magazine requirements. An author starts with the hope, and probably with the belief, that his own theme-idea is a good one. He should not try to find reasons to buttress his opinion. He should look for reasons why his theme-idea may be a poor one, and then try to evaluate such reasons, see if they are valid or if they can be overcome.

Writers-in-training often feel strongly that they must write only about a theme-idea that interests them. This is perhaps a matter of personality. Certainly interest is the great driving force in any writer's career. If a writer dislikes cooking and does not especially care about food, he had better not write a cookbook or even an article about food. However, the professional manages to become interested in a broad range of subjects. The writer-in-training should be able to get excited about all kinds of theme-ideas. If he cannot, perhaps writing is not his forte.

A second statement often made is that a writer should write only about what he knows. The true statement is that he should know a great deal about what he writes. He can acquire the knowledge through live and library research.

Writers-in-training continually go to editors and ask: "Have you any ideas for articles?" The author is really asking the editor if he has a theme-idea which the author can develop and write, and which the editor will ultimately buy. In the first place, no editor is so constructive, so original, so imaginative that he can supply his magazine with all its theme-ideas. Secondly, a theme-idea only becomes valid as it is developed through research. It isn't something you can grab out of the air or take from the lips of an editor. Editors are not researchers; writers must do their own work. Nine out of ten theme-ideas for articles are developed by authors. They are developed through the process described in this chapter. Editors have not the time nor the training to go through the process of finding theme-ideas.

Occasionally editors do suggest the nucleus of an idea or even a theme-idea. The suggestion is usually made to a writer who is an expert in the subject area. For example, Wolfgang Langewiesche is one of the ablest airplane writers in the country. Having flown his own plane for years, and having read immensely about airplanes, he is steeped in live and library research of the air. Suppose an editor gets the nucleus of an idea: the difficulties of landing a plane by instrument in heavy fog. Langewiesche can develop a theme-idea and an outline in his mind without doing further research. He can draw upon the research material he has absorbed in past years. Suppose Langewiesche were asked to develop a theme-idea in the area of garbage dumps. Here he would have to do live and library research before he could come up with a valid theme-idea or a valid outline or an adequate finished piece.

Suggesting the nucleus of an idea or a theme-idea to a writer ignorant of the subject is of little value, and most writers who ask editors for "ideas" just show their own ignorance. A writer who understands how theme-ideas and outlines are developed, whether his understanding is instinctive or conscious, knows that an editor cannot do the writer's job.

The inability to obtain good theme-ideas is a major cause of failure in the writing trade. If an author perseveres with a second-rate theme-idea, he just wastes his time. If he writes six articles based upon poor theme-ideas, his writing career will probably end from discouragement.

At times a writer's career will start with a big success, and then die because the author has not learned what good theme-ideas are and how to obtain them. In the winter of 1961 an agent approached a newspaper woman whom the government was training to be a lady astronaut. The woman could put words together, had written a number of feature articles for newspaper supplements, but had little success with any substantial market. An agent gave her the assignment to write an article on the problems she went through in her government training to be a possible space passenger. The material was fresh, the theme-idea adequate, and the author completed an acceptable piece. Due to the exclusiveness of the material, the piece was sold to *McCall's* magazine for the unusually high price of $5000. The author thought she was made as a writer; she was unmade. She wrote on assorted subjects a dozen articles, none of which were good. This woman could write, but she had never learned how to find the nucleus of an idea and develop it through research into a good theme-idea. She knew much about the later steps in writing, but had never acquired skill with the first step, namely how to find a good theme-idea.

2

PROBLEMS OF RESEARCH AND ORGANIZATION

The writer-in-training has now selected his subject matter and has developed a theme-idea. The theme-idea has been tested in relation to published pieces and seems worthwhile. Library research is continued in an intensive fashion. The author takes notes. His purpose is to appropriate for his own use facts other writers have gathered, points of view other writers have portrayed. Everything that has been previously published is available.

Authors get unduly worried about using other authors' copyrighted material. What is a copyright? When an original piece of writing is first published in the United States, the publisher prints a copyright notice in connection with the piece and deposits a copy of the printed matter with the Library of Congress, paying a nominal fee. This copyrights the work. For twenty-eight years no one can republish the work without permission. At the end of twenty-eight years, upon the payment of another fee, the copyright can be renewed for a second twenty-eight-year period. Fifty-six years after first publication the work goes into the public domain, and anyone can use or reprint the piece without permission.

In Great Britain and many other foreign countries a similar procedure is followed, but the copyright remains in force until fifty years after the author's death. This creates anomalies. For instance, Henry James published *Washington Square* in 1880. It went out of copyright in the United States fifty-six years later, or in 1936. However, since Henry James did not die until 1916, his novel will remain in copyright in England until 1966.

A writer cannot quote from copyrighted material without permission, which usually means that he has to pay an agreed-upon fee to the holder of the copyright. A writer cannot use someone else's words exactly or slightly changed. Likewise, a writer cannot condense someone else's composition or copy someone else's organization of facts or of ideas. Doing any of the above is not doing one's own work; it is stealing. The writer who does this because a plagiarist and can be prosecuted under the law. The cardinal principle is that a writer's work must be his own.

However, there is no copyright on facts as such or on ideas as such or on a point of view towards a fact. The date of President Kennedy's birth or of his war service can be used by anyone. The first man to say that all men are mortal or that trees do not die of old age is granted no exclusiveness to these ideas through copyright. On any one subject matter there may be dozens of articles or books. The same facts and the same ideas appear over and over again in printed matter. Each book or article, even though on the same subject, is told with different words, different paragraphs, and is organized in a different way, so that no two pieces are alike.

No writer should be a plagiarist, but avoiding plagiarism is easy. The problem for the writer-in-training is to learn how to acquire from others. Mark Twain in his autobiography tells how he wrote a dedication for his book *Innocents Abroad*. To his horror he discovered that he had used verbatim the dedication that Oliver Wendell Holmes had written and published in connection with a book of his own verse. Mark Twain had read this book of Holmes's verse many times and had unconsciously absorbed the exact wording of Holmes's dedication. Mark Twain wrote to Holmes, apologizing at length. Then Mark Twain tells of how Holmes

> . . . laughed the kindest and healingest laugh over the whole matter and at considerable length and in happy phrase assured Twain that there was no crime in unconscious plagiarism; that he

(Holmes) committed it every day, that he (Twain) committed it every day, that every man alive on the earth who writes or speaks commits it every day, and not merely once or twice but every time he opens his mouth; that all our phrasings are spiritualized shadows cast multitudinously from our readings; that no happy phrase of ours is ever quite original with us; there is nothing of our own in it except some slight change born of our temperament, character, environment, teachings, and associations; that this slight change differentiates it from another man's manner of saying it, stamps it with our special style, and makes it our own for the time being; all the rest of it being old, moldy, antique, and smelling of the breath of a thousand generations of them that have used it before.

Holmes in the above is telling Mark Twain how one writer must of necessity borrow from another. No one is an effective writer who has not learned to use other people's writings. An author's work is derivative. Writing deals with facts and thought in a progression out of the past. One writer carries the torch, and then the next picks it up and carries it farther.

When Mark Twain quoted Holmes's dedication verbatim, Twain was in the wrong. The fact that the copying was unconscious does not save him. However, the Twain-Holmes point of view is sound and essential. Facts ascertained by one writer are available for the next. Points of view towards these facts are open to all. A writer can be against sin or against a particular sin regardless of how many clergymen have preceded him with the same point of view.

How much or how deeply can a writer use the work of others? The theme-idea is the determining factor. The theme-idea guides the writer as to what facts are selected, what points of view are used. A writer absorbs what other writers have written. Then when he spews it forth, guided by his own theme-idea and his own personality, the result becomes his own. If the theme-idea is or has truly become the author's own, if it determines what is used from the written material of others, there is no danger of plagiarism. If the writer's theme-idea is not his own, if it is identical with the theme-idea of a published piece, the writer will be in grave danger of plagiarism.

The danger of most writers-in-training is not one of possible plagiarism. They are more likely to err in failing to sufficiently immerse themselves in the facts and thought of others so as to point up and enrich their own composition.

Perhaps another way of making this clear is to ask the reader to consider the following: Paul Reynolds has written a book which the reader is now reading. In this book Reynolds has quoted from Mark Twain's autobiography. He has given credit for the quotation. He has not obtained permission to quote because the autobiography is no longer in copyright. Reynolds has repudiated the implication in the Twain-Holmes incident that it is all right unconsciously to quote verbatim without permission. When the material is in copyright, Reynolds asserts, such action is wrong and illegal, whether conscious or unconscious. However, Reynolds has quoted the basic thesis, and then has restated it in his own words with his own qualifications. Reynolds discovered the Twain-Holmes incident in the course of his own library research. His use of it is determined by his own theme-idea. In the Appendix of this volume are verbatim reprints of three previously published articles. Here Reynolds had to obtain permission. He paid a fee satisfactory to the owners of the pieces for the right to reprint. In two of the cases the original authors are paid; in the third case, the widow of the original author.

We have been speaking of library research. Live research is also conducted to acquire facts and points of view. A major part of live research is interviewing people who played a part in what the author is writing about or who are experts on the subject. However, before the interview the author should have done his homework. Library research will help the author prepare good questions from which further information will result. Also, an expert will talk and answer questions more readily to a person who exhibits some knowledge of the expert's field.

Many authors take notes as they interview. Some avoid this because people will often talk more freely if they are not conscious of the interrogator taking notes. A few authors have tried tape recorders, but usually find they inhibit people from talking freely. A few writers have a recorder hidden in their clothes so that the subject does not know that what he is saying is being taped.

The most lowly writers-in-training can often obtain interviews even with very prominent people. A letter to the president of a corporation, or an important scientist, or a labor leader, telling who the author is, what he is trying to do, and requesting an interview, will often receive an affirmative response. Telling the person in advance that the author will take only fifteen minutes of his time, and sticking to fifteen minutes, will help. An author who keeps within his allotted time can usually obtain a second interview later on, should that be desirable. Usually an author does not want facts from a prominent person; these he can obtain elsewhere. He wants comment or an explanation. Talking to people who are not prominent, such as firemen who have fought a fire in a garbage dump, should be done in as informal a manner as possible. Some writers prefer bars, and spend much expense money buying witnesses drinks. Many like to go to a person's home. Occasionally an interview with a celebrity can be informal. President Theodore Roosevelt once granted an interview while he was shaving. The President said that that was one time when he had nothing else to do. The reporter found this quite satisfactory.

An author may want to show his finished piece to one or more of the people he has interviewed. This does not mean that there is going to be censorship. The author needn't change any point of view or ideas, but he wants to check on the accuracy of his factual statements. In the case of direct quotations, verbal accuracy is a must, and nearly always the author should verify the quotation.

Both library and live research are essential for effective non-fiction writing. Although much library research should precede live research, the two should nevertheless be intermingled. The library prepares for live research. Live research opens new vistas which send the author back to the library. Newspaper men are often unsuccessful in the magazine field because they have not learned to undertake and mingle library research with live research. Elderly people often have trouble in writing because they find live research difficult, and therefore do chiefly library research. Amateurs often fail because they do insufficient research of either kind.

Editors or agents will sometimes ask a writer if he enjoys research. Research is, of course, work, but it has an interest somewhat akin to the work of a detective. The author is continually trying to track down the source and to substantiate some elusive, alleged fact. Research also has the charm of the unexpected. The author of the article on the Battle of Atlanta may have been completely surprised to discover through his library research that it was a battle fought by boys. The writer investigating plankton had probably never heard of the aqua-therm. He is intrigued and the richer for his knowledge. Research has its charms for many. A person who does not enjoy it is going to dislike a large and essential part of non-fiction writing.

How much research should an author do? There is no dogmatic answer. It is sometimes said that an author should obtain at least twice as many facts, anecdotes, and opinions as he will need for the completed piece. From one point of view all writing is a matter of selection and rejection. The more material the writer has, the better his selection can be and the better the final piece.

The author has a guide for his piece in his theme-idea, but he very soon needs a more detailed guide, namely an outline. A tentative outline may be prepared as soon as the theme-idea has been definitely developed and accepted. Or it may be prepared during the library research. Usually it is prepared before doing the live research.

This outline is to guide the author. It is not written for editors. It will show what the piece will contain and the order of the contents. It will suggest how the piece will open and how it will end. It will suggest roughly the progression of the piece. The theme-idea is the general guide as to what the author will search for in his library and live research; the outline is the specific guide. Outlining a piece is organizing it. Writers-in-training often fail to understand that effective writing depends upon good organization, perhaps because critics and book reviewers seldom comment on this. Winston Churchill is a magnificent non-fiction writer. People comment on his material, his colorful phrases, and his insight. Part of his excellence is due to the organization of his material. Everyone has listened to poor speeches, and the comment is often made that the speaker rambled along. The speaker has failed to effectively organize his material.

The organization of sentences in each paragraph will be discussed later. The outline is a guide to the organization of the paragraphs. If a good outline has been prepared, the paragraphs, when written, will be in their proper position in the pattern. If the piece is to be told chronologically, the pattern of a chronological outline is easy to follow. Perhaps the piece opens in the present, then a flashback, and then back to the present. Perhaps the piece attempts to prove a premise; then the outline should indicate a sequence to the various proofs. Perhaps the piece is an account of a plane disaster; then the outline may show the paragraphs in such order as to show mounting horror. One of the articles printed in the Supplement to this book is followed by an outline prepared by myself. A student might try changing the order of the paragraphs to show how the pattern would be broken. The most that can be said at this stage is that every article should have a pattern, so that when the paragraphs are written, there will be a reason for the position of each paragraph in the piece.

An outline may be of any length. It may be a couple of paragraphs; it may cover every detail of each paragraph of the completed piece, and in itself be as long as the final piece will be. Most authors start with a very short outline, then expand and revise it as they do their research.

The opening of an article should catch the attention of the reader. Many an after-dinner speaker opens his address with a joke. He wants to catch the attention and interest of his audience. An article does not usually start with a joke (unless it is a humorous piece), but it should catch the reader's attention. In his research the author has been looking for a good opening for his piece. Perhaps he discovered that the garbage dump is infested with rats. If he interviewed a boy who claimed that he shot seventeen rats in the dump one Saturday morning, the piece might start:

> On Saturday morning, July 17th, Johnnie Bradshaw, fifteen years old, shot seventeen rats in a vacant half-acre of land in the middle of Athens, Idaho. This vacant half-acre is the town garbage dump, the blight of Athens.

Now the outline may just begin as a note: "Opening: Johnnie Bradshaw shooting rats." Or it may start with the sentence above.

Here is the opening of the article on the Battle of Atlanta:

> Atlanta was a young man's battle, fought on the shank end of an old, bitter war. About a quarter of the Union soldiers who closed in on "the Gate City of the South" on July 22, 1864, were 19 or younger. Another quarter were no more than 21. And of the 50,000 Confederate defenders of the battered, panic-stricken town, 35,000 were 21 or younger. Scattered through both forces were boys of 13, 14 or 15.

The writer does not start off his article by telling us who won the battle, or how many casualties there were, or how important the outcome was to the North. He starts out to interest us with something that most people probably were not aware of, namely the youth of the soldiers.

The outline will also suggest a possible ending. In writing about "The Blight of the Athens Garbage Dump" the author may look for an ending that suggests a possible solution. Research may have dug up the fact that there is a single Republican member of the Athens city council, and perhaps the author will plan to end his piece with a quote from this councilman as to a solution of the dump troubles. Or perhaps the author will imagine an ending which will echo the opening, namely a final reference to the rats. Perhaps a housewife maintains that, despite the seventeen rats the boy shot, the dump is just as infested as ever with rats.

The opening of the article "New York's New Queen of Fashion" is as follows:

One of the more engaging intercontinental love affairs of the century thus far has been that of Paris-born Pauline Trigère, now an eminent fashion designer, and the United States of America.

The end of the article echoes the beginning:

A naturalized American since 1942, Pauline makes one or two trips to France each year to buy fabrics. Every time she arrives in Paris she suffers a twinge of nostalgia, but soon recovers from it.

"I'll love Paris always," she said, on returning from her latest voyage. "But honestly, the lively pace of America is so exciting that sometimes I think it was made just for me."

An author's outline, as well as suggesting the opening and the ending, will suggest the material for the body of the piece. For the garbage dump theme-idea an author may write down an outline in note form such as the following:

1. Opening with anecdote of shooting rats.
2. Description of the dump: size, amount of garbage delivered each day, estimated total amount of garbage in dump.
3. Number of houses nearby; what owners say as to smell, rats, smoke.

4. Health menace; statement from Board of Health, from doctors.
5. Dump reduces property values. (Author's note: Can I get such evidence and will it be dull?)
6. History of the dump. How long has it been in existence? Why did it start? Has it become more of a blight as it grew larger?
7. Why does the dump catch on fire? Interviews about this, with quotes from neighbors and from firemen who have fought fires in the dump.
8. What do other nearby communities do with their garbage?
9. What is likely to happen in the future? Interview with the mayor of Athens and also with the head garbage collector.
10. What should be done to end the blight? Quote from the lone Republican on the City Council as to the need for an incinerator.

Now, the above is by no means a final outline or a good outline. It is more notes prepared by an author before he has done most of his research work. As he does his research his outline will change. Perhaps the volunteer firemen objected to fighting a fire in the dump. They said their wives objected to the muck they got on their clothes and shoes. Here perhaps the author can get a good anecdote. Perhaps the author discovers that the owner of the land, on which the garbage is being dumped, wanted the land filled in, and hence wants the dump there. Perhaps the owner of the land is a local Democratic politician; if so, the author may get some political overtones into his piece. Perhaps the Republican member of the city council will say nothing; hence, the author's suggested ending is no good. Perhaps the author will want to add a couple of paragraphs of alternative sites for a dump. Perhaps the author will convince himself that machines could be installed so as to make the garbage into fertilizer and that, by so doing, the city in the end would save money and help agriculture. Any of the above will require alterations in the outline. Here is a much shorter outline prepared by a professional writer after he has got his theme-idea but before he has done more than perhaps a half hour of library research.

SUBJECT: The recently developed electronic machine, called the "pacemaker," which restores and maintains normal heart rhythm in individuals suffering from a heart disease known as the Stokes-Adams Syndrone.

THEME: Present and future use of the pacemaker.

OPENING: An anecdotal record of how the pacemaker was used for the first time in a human being.

WHAT THE ARTICLE IS ABOUT:
The development of pacemakers, experiments with them, and explanations of their effectiveness.

ENDING: Prediction of the future use of the pacemaker and the summation of achievement to date in terms of actual lives saved.

We have described the process of gathering material and organizing it, which requires a tentative outline, and then revisions and expansions of the outline. There may be several outlines before the final one. Do most professional article writers follow such a procedure? Most of them prepare at least one typed outline. Some type revised ones. Some keep the revisions in their heads. A few never prepare an outline but keep the entire organization of the piece in their heads. William Prescott, the historian, half blind, kept the organization of a chapter in his mind, would then prepare in his mind the actual composition, would memorize his own sentences so that he could dictate an entire chapter at a time from memory. But most people are not Prescotts. For the writer-in-training a method of work is important. Effective article writing requires the gathering of material, a good selection of what is gathered, and a careful organization of what is selected. One's mind must get into the habit of making selections and rejections, the habit of seeing material in an organized form, the habit of continually searching for superior material and superior organization. Once these habits have become ingrained, the extent to which outlines and their revisions are typed out becomes a matter of the author's convenience.

3

REWRITING—THE PROBLEMS OF REVISION

The writer has now developed the nucleus of an idea into a theme-idea, has done his library and live research, and has outlined his piece. His voluminous notes are before him. He starts writing. Some professionals write their first drafts in a white heat without pausing for revision. Any pause for corrections causes them to lose their "first fine careless rapture." Other writers revise and eliminate as they put their first draft on paper. Whether with some revision or not, the first draft of a completed article results. The author is apt to read over this first draft and congratulate himself on how well the pages read, how unusual the contents are. It is natural to like what has been done. The writer worked hard. He started at the beginning and ended at the end. He put words together according to his preference. The professional writer, however, makes himself study his first draft manuscript critically. Often he becomes appalled at how ineffective the pages are, how badly they are written. This second-thought realization of a manuscript's weakness is not discouraging. It is a challenge driving him on to revise. The professional and the amateur writer differ in that the professional has learned how essential revision is; the professional rewrites and improves.

A few people can sit down at their typewriters and write, off the top of their heads, the first version of a piece, and with such a manuscript have a moderate success. They may sell first drafts to the minor markets. Such writers get no better, advance no further. Typical newspaper reporting is competent and professional; little else. Newspaper men rarely rewrite. Their copy is printed the day it is written and there is no time. For the free-lance professional writer success with the high-paying magazines, success with books, any real success with the written word requires extensive revision, extensive rewriting.

The writer-in-training has to learn to rewrite. He has to learn to judge his own prose as if it was someone else's, ascertain where it is weak, where it drags, where it is dull. It is not easy to acquire this habit. Some writers put a piece aside for a few days so that they can look at it more aloofly. This is a practical method with fiction but more difficult with an article. The subject matter of an article may be timely or an editor may have given an author a deadline. Under any circumstances there is a need to get on with the job. However, the writer-in-training, regardless of the time schedule, must acquire the knack of discovering his own imperfections. He should study his first draft on the basis of the following questions:

1. Is all the material in the piece related to the basic theme-idea?
2. Will the reader remember the theme-idea?
3. Will the piece seem important to the reader?
4. Is the piece well organized?
5. Is there sufficient variety of material?
6. Are there paragraphs which are dull?
7. Is there too much repetition or too much repetition of effect?
8. Are there a sufficient number of good anecdotes, ones that in each case illustrate a point without straining?
9. Is every paragraph in the piece absolutely clear?
10. Does the piece have "pace," does it keep moving, keep intriguing the reader?
11. The opening and the ending, are they both effective?
12. Are there paragraphs that are underwritten and need amplification?

13. Are there sentences or paragraphs which could be shortened or eliminated without losing much?
14. Are there places where more factual material would help? Sentences which should be more specific?
15. Are there paragraphs which are too emotional or too cute?
16. Is there any doubt as to the truth of any sentence which states a fact?

Most of the above questions have been in the author's mind from the time of the development of the theme-idea. Now the author asks himself: are the questions satisfactorily answered by the word on paper? Theoretically the first draft could be in such good shape that all the above questions could be answered in the affirmative. In such a case the first draft would be a satisfactory final version. In practice this rarely occurs. We are dealing with matters of degree, and matters of degree are nearly always subject to improvement. Also, it is difficult to answer the questions except on the basis of a manuscript which can be viewed as a whole.

Some writers can develop a satisfactory piece with one revision. This means that they find satisfactory answers to all the questions in one rewriting. Because of the number of the questions few writers seem able to do this all at once. Hence there usually is a third, a fourth, and even further drafts. The number seems to depend upon the writer and his habits of work. The English historian G. M. Trevelyan usually found four drafts necessary. The Pulitzer prize winner Conrad Richter often prepares as many as ten drafts. Perhaps three or four is the average. Margery Allingham made the following statement:

> I write every paragraph four times—once to get my meaning down, once to put in anything I have left out, once to take out anything that seems unnecessary, and once to make the whole thing sound as if I had only just thought of it.

With most writers different paragraphs and different pages in a piece present different problems. One page may stand as it was in the first draft with scarcely a verbal change. Another two pages may be intermingled, switched around, and revised as many as ten times.

On the basis of the first draft the professional writer proceeds to rewrite with the specific questions consciously or unconsciously in mind. Practice and experience have caused him to absorb the questions. The writer-in-training should probably study each question specifically.

1. Is all the material in the piece related to the basic theme-idea?

There may be facts or ideas in the manuscript that have little relation to the original theme-idea. In the *Reader's Digest* article "A Seat Belt Could Save Your Life" the theme-idea is that an automobile driver should use a seat belt for safety. Perhaps the author of this article in his first draft wrote about the safety factor of seat belts in airplanes. Then in a later draft he discards such material because his original theme-idea encompassed automobile seat belts only. In the proposed article on "The Blight of the Athens Garbage Dump" perhaps there are paragraphs dealing with the history of the dump. The writer must ask himself if this material has sufficient relation to the blight, to the theme-idea. When preparing the outline and doing the research, the history seemed necessary. Perhaps now, looking at the piece as a whole, the only history needed is a sentence as to when the dump was started. All else about the history is eliminated. Or perhaps the dump has always been a blight and the history is needed to show how the blight has been getting worse and worse. In this case the history may be germane to the original theme-idea.

2. Will the reader remember the theme-idea?

Usually a statement in an article must be repeated at least three times for the reader to remember it. An author may, for emphasis, repeat the same words. Usually he sneaks up on the reader's memory. He says the same thing in different ways with different words. In examining a first draft an author must ask himself: is the theme-idea repeated enough so that the reader will remember it? The *Reader's Digest* article "A Seat Belt Could Save Your Life" is approximately 1200 words in length. The theme-idea of this short article is expressed in the title, and then repeated, at least by implication, in the 4th, 7th, 8th, 9th, and 10th paragraphs. In an article on "The Blight of the Athens Garbage Dump," the material must be concentrated on the blight if the reader is going to remember the theme-idea. In the case of most articles, in one way or another, the theme-idea must be repeated so that there is no possibility of the reader's forgetting it.

3. Will the piece seem important to the reader?

There was a basic importance to the theme-idea or the author would not have selected and developed it. However, does it read sufficiently important? The health menace makes the blight of the garbage dump important. Perhaps there is only a paragraph on what the Board of Health has said about the health menace. Can this be expanded? When did the agent for the Board of Health visit the dump? What about earlier visits? Would the Department elaborate on their statement. Why not obtain statements from local doctors as to a possible health menace? Such material should make the piece seem more important. Then again, perhaps there is some other town or small city where disease was directly traced to a garbage dump. The author may be able to suggest that Athens is likely to have the same unhappy experience.

4. Is the piece well organized?

The writer has followed his outline, his piece follows a logical plan, and should on the whole be satisfactorily organized. However, examining the fabric as a written article, minor alterations in the organization may be required. In "The Blight of the Athens Garbage Dump," material about the dumps in two neighboring cities ran consecutively in the outline and is together in the first draft. In general, material about the same kind of thing should be in consecutive paragraphs. But if one city illustrates one point and the other city another, it may be better to separate the account of one city from the other.

There may be a paragraph which advances the article and has been put in one position in the piece. The same paragraph may also be supporting evidence for some allegation which might suggest another place for it in the piece. For instance, there may be a paragraph on how the smoke and stench can be smelt one half mile away from the dump. Perhaps this paragraph in the outline followed an account of a fire in the dump and hence is in this position in the first draft. But if the Board of Health stated that there was only a serious health menace if smoke and stench was smelt at least one quarter of a mile away from the dump, the author may want to change the position of the paragraph; he may want it to follow the Board of Health statement and not follow the account of the fire.

5. Is there sufficient variety of material?

If there is not, and the author's research notes will not solve the problem, the author must try and think of vistas of research which have not been probed and go out and get more material. Perhaps in the garbage dump article the statements from citizens about the blight are all too similar. Here the solution may be to get greater variety of statements. Perhaps the local clergyman or an old-timer who reached manhood before the dump started would add variety. Perhaps a statement favoring the dump's existence would be a change of pace and add spice to the piece.

6. Are there paragraphs which are dull?

Dullness should usually just be eliminated. Sometimes this is not practicable. There may be one or more paragraphs which give the reader information essential for his comprehension of the theme-idea and premise. Due to the outline this information is packed all together in one section of the piece. If these purely informative pages lag in interest, it may be wise to scatter the information throughout the piece.

7. Is there too much repetition or too much repetition in effect?

Direct repetition is where an author says the same thing more than once in the same words or in pretty similar words. There may be a need to repeat for emphasis or for cumulative emotion or just to hammer some point home. Hence the same words or slightly different words are used for emphasis. However, an author should question all direct repetition. The elimination is easy. The author just removes what is repetitious, inserting a connecting word or sentence.

Repetition in effect occurs where two different episodes or descriptions illustrate the same point. If the point is relatively unimportant, one of the anecdotes or descriptions should be omitted. If the point is important, is the vital point in the article, the author may purposely want repetition in effect. In "A Seat Belt Could Save Your Life" there are two descriptions of automobile accidents without seat belts, four descriptions with seat belts, and one description where some of the occupants used seat belts and some did not. Here the repetitions in effect are purposeful; the author is driving home his theme.

8. Are there a sufficient number of good anecdotes, ones that in each case illustrate a point without straining?

Non-fiction is more readable if it contains good anecdotes which illustrate points the author is making. Anecdotes are often a requisite for the successful magazine article. If there are not enough in the piece, an author should go through his notes for more, and possibly search for more in further research. Quotations from well-known people are not in themselves anecdotes, but one or two may be used in a pinch. Perhaps Bartlett has a quotation about garbage which would be apropos in the article about "The Blight of the Athens Garbage Dump." Jokes are usually too remote from the subject for their use to be warranted. There is often a fine line between an anecdote and a joke. The author is not trying to be funny. Whatever is used must have a direct relation to the piece. It should be an illustration or evidence of something said in the piece.

9. Is every paragraph in the piece absolutely clear?

Clarity of writing always improves an article. Because the author has become somewhat of an expert on a subject, he may say things which are clear to himself but aren't clear to a reader uninformed about the subject. In general, it is wise to assume that the reader is intelligent but grossly ignorant. Lack of clarity may be due to not telling the reader facts or relationships which are essential for him to know if he is to understand the article. Often lack of clarity is just due to writing atrocious English. This problem of good English will be discussed in the next chapter.

10. Does the piece have "pace," does it keep moving, keep intriguing the reader?

It is hard for a teacher to help a writer with this, and writers often find it difficult to know what "pace" is, or to know what they can do to improve in this respect. If the reader can stop reading in the middle of a piece, if the reader has absorbed everything to be said in the article in the first half, something is wrong. The typical front-page newspaper story reports in capsule form in the first paragraph or two the basic facts that happened. Further paragraphs enlarge on what has already been told. A magazine article should not unfold the entire story until almost the last paragraph, even though the theme-idea and the point of view are made explicit early in the piece.

> 11. The opening and the ending, are they both effective?

The author has been experimenting with leads from the very start, but he may still want to experiment. One of his best anecdotes may make a better lead. The same may be true of the end. Perhaps the author will want to write a different end in order to echo the opening or in order to repeat the theme-idea. Perhaps the article about "The Blight of the Athens Garbage Dump" ends with a statement from the lone Republican Councilman telling what he thinks should be done about the dump. However, the author may have in his notes an interview with the mother of the boy who shot seventeen rats. The mother may have stated that she did not approve of her boy shooting animals, but she may have said: "The rats in this dump are such a curse and such a health hazard, that my husband and I have agreed to pay for all the bullets used shooting rats in the dump." This may echo the opening of the article, and the author may think it will make a good end. He will then insert in the middle of the piece the Republican Councilman's statement, or possibly eliminate it altogether.

> 12. Are there paragraphs which are underwritten and need amplification?

There may be a sentence which could be dramatized, even though this would require using a paragraph. In the seventh paragraph of the *Reader's Digest* article "A Seat Belt Could Save Your Life" the author might have stated that Charles Pulse owed his life to a safety belt. Instead, the author dramatized the incident. Sometimes a statement of fact needs amplification in that it needs verification. The sixth paragraph of the seat-belt article opens with the sentence: "Years of research at Cornell University, at the University of California and elsewhere, and analysis of the accident records of 22 states have confirmed the usefulness of ordinary lap-type belts." This paragraph could have ended here. Instead, the author added verification in further sentences.

> 13. Are there sentences or paragraphs which could be shortened or eliminated without losing much?

Most writers overwrite, and cutting improves their piece. One form of cutting is the removal of individual words. Another way is to reconstruct a sentence. An author can often find a direct, simple sentence to replace one with conditional phrases. Another form of cutting is that of condensation. There is a long paragraph. Is it needed? Does it advance the piece? Is it interesting? If in one or two sentences a writer finds that he can give the gist of a paragraph, he probably had better do so. Finally, cutting can be the removal of some of the material, and the elimination of the paragraphs which deal with this material. Often the author says too much. Just because there is no limit to how much an author can put into a piece, there is a danger of putting in more than is really needed to carry out the theme-idea. The elimination of superfluous words will be discussed in a later chapter.

> 14. Are there places where more factual material would help? Are there sentences which should be more specific?

Most authors, when they read over their first draft, find some holes in their research. There may be a dozen places where facts would strengthen the piece. Some of the missing facts may be in the author's notes; some he will have to gather through further research. In the article "New York's

New Queen of Fashion" it is mentioned that dresses are priced at $19.95. The exact price is more effective than saying the dresses were highly priced or cheaply priced. In the proposed garbage dump article perhaps the age of the boy who shot the rats was mentioned. Of course, the author can cheat and just say he was a young boy, but it will be a better piece if it mentions that he was a 15-year-old boy.

15. Are there paragraphs which are too emotional or too cute?

Many writers have a tendency to be lyrical. Often the writer's favorite passage, an emotional paragraph, is the poorest. In "A Seat Belt Could Save Your Life" the author gets emotional at the start and gets away with it, but the writer-in-training should beware. Let the facts carry their own emotion. Beware of editorializing, personalizing, and emotionalizing. Likewise, beware of being too cute. A sentence which might be recognized as being clever should be eliminated. An author is not writing to exhibit his cleverness.

16. Is there any doubt as to the truth of any sentence which states a fact?

The author may have made a statement in his piece which he believes is true, but is he certain? People he interviewed can lie or be inaccurate. An author is not excused because he inadvertently repeated a lie. Likewise, published matter can be inaccurate. The author can misread, or just make a foolish mistake. For every statement, important or trivial, the author should check and evaluate his evidence. This may result in changes in his copy without further research or because of further research.

Here is an example of an extraordinary misfortune that came to the author as a result of a factual error.

A writer sold to *The Saturday Evening Post* an article on the everyday life of a man billed as "the loneliest man in America." The subject of the article lived in a house close to the Union Pacific railway tracks in the Nevada desert. His job was in connection with the railroad. His nearest neighbor was twenty miles away. Supplies, mail, messages reached him via a conductor of a train making unscheduled stops. The author of the article stated that there was no tree within a mile of the house. The author had visited the house in the course of his live research but he had failed to notice a large eucalyptus tree in the back yard. A photographer sent by the *Post* took a side-view picture of the house showing the tree. The article with the statement of no trees and the photograph with a tree got into print before the discrepancy was discovered. The author was caught, through a photograph. The *Post* refused to buy any further articles from this author, and he lost thousands of dollars in future sales he could not make.

Most of the general, popular magazines with a national circulation have a research department to check on statements of fact made in articles they have purchased. However, such magazines still must depend upon their authors for fundamental truthfulness, and they have a suspicion and prejudice against authors whom they catch in a mistake. Non-fiction which disregards the truth is meaningless. It is unimportant whether there was a tree close to the home of "the loneliest man in America," but if an author makes mistakes with the unimportant, who knows what mistakes he may make with the important? Factual accuracy is essential. The search for the truth is a way of mind without which the entire fabric of one's non-fiction falls to pieces.

The preceding analysis of the sixteen questions, the analysis of the problems of revision, is of limited help to the writer-in-training. What is presented as an answer may be begging the question or may be suggesting further questions which remain unanswered. It has been stated, for instance, that in any article there must be a sufficient variety of material, a sufficient number of good anecdotes, no dull paragraphs. The writer-in-training will ask how much variety is sufficient, how many anecdotes, when is a paragraph dull? One can answer that all depends upon the particular article, but such a reply is of no help. Anyone trying to teach writing, whether by book or in person, can only be of partial aid. Perhaps the best solution for the unanswerable questions is to lead the writer-in-training back to where we started, to the theme-idea. This is the determining force for the research, for the outline, for the writing of the first draft, and for the rewriting. This is the control. If the theme-idea for an article is sound, if it has grown in the conscious and subconscious mind, if the writer-in-training has acquired the theme-idea method of work through practice and habit, the unanswerable questions will not loom so large, and to a certain extent they will answer themselves.

It is natural and a common occurrence for a writer-in-training to get discouraged. He writes manuscripts and they are rejected. The process of learning described thus far seems long and slow, and the writer-in-training sees little sign of progress. He wonders if a critic could tell him how to make a manuscript salable. In the writers' magazines he read advertisements of self-styled critics who will read a script for a fee and tell the author what is wrong. Beguiling as these advertisements are with their glowing testimonials, these advertising quacks are of no help. There is no successful method of telling an author how to turn a bad manuscript into a good one. If editors could tell an author this, they would do so. The object of an editor is to obtain good manuscripts in any way possible. What an editor cannot do, a self-styled critic cannot do.

The author of this volume has never known of a professional writer who felt that in his apprenticeship he was helped by one of these advertising critics. One reason for the failure of the advertising critic is that he is usually unqualified. His editorial experience and know-how are inadequate. The fundamental reason for the critic's inability to help is that the critic is operating on an unsound basis. Learning to write comprises learning a process and a technique over a continuous period of time. It is learning through trial and error. When help is possible, it is by continuous overall instruction. It involves all the factors described in the previous chapters. A poor writer is seldom turned into a better one through obtaining specific criticism of one or several scripts.

It is difficult to convince the writer-in-training of this. Usually he discovers the uselessness of the critic by paying the fees until money or patience runs out. Here is a suggestion. Suppose the writer-in-training sends his manuscript to an advertising critic. The critic will ask for a fee by return mail. Suppose the writer replies that he cannot pay a fee, but that he will follow the critic's editorial suggestions and give the critic 50 percent of the money received from a sale. As no fee-charging critic will entertain such a proposition, the author may realize that the fee-charging critic is engaged in a racket.

The process described in the last three chapters, that of developing an idea, doing live and library research, outlining, doing the actual writing, and finally completing the revision, all of this is work which is intermingled and jumbled together. No two writers work in the same way, and any one writer may vary his procedure from piece to piece. Nevertheless, the intermingling of the work is a characteristic of the professional and one of the factors in success.

Writers who compartmentalize, first develop a theme-idea, then research a piece, then write, and then revise, often lose a lot. A theme-idea not developed through research and writing often becomes inflexible. When the research and the writing are separated, the research, coming first, may guide the writing, but the writing does not guide the research. Vistas which the writing may suggest are not explored in the research, for the research has been done. A lack of some fact or of a point of view, or a hole in one's research, tends not to be plugged, but rather the author walks around his lack and avoids what is required for his best accomplishment. Because one can write and revise regardless of one's ignorance, it is easy to complete a piece while still ignorant. A piece written and revised in a compartmentalized fashion may be good enough for publication; it is seldom the author's best. A writer has to learn each step and then learn to intermingle all the steps.

4

THE PROBLEM OF WRITING GOOD ENGLISH

When writers-in-training deliver a manuscript to an editor, they often ask if their style is satisfactory. Editors can rarely give an adequate answer to such a question; editors do not think in terms of style. They do want clear effective English. Clear, effective English depends upon:

1. A well-organized piece (discussed in Chapter 2).
2. Well-organized individual paragraphs.
3. Sentences which are clear and easily understood.
4. Sentences which are forceful.
5. Sentences which are colorful.
6. Variety of sentence structure.
7. Effective choice of individual words with emphasis on the simple word in lieu of the pretentious, and with emphasis on the strong verb.

An author who masters the above seven problems need not be concerned with any problems of style. In all probability he will develop through the years a distinctive style of his own, but it is unimportant whether he does or not. The writer-in-training's problem with any style is the problem of writing clear, effective English.

Effective writing requires effective organization. Just as an entire article can be poorly organized, so can individual paragraphs. A paragraph should have unity. Its first sentence is often its lead sentence. Further sentences may substantiate the statement made in the lead sentence, or they may be modifications or expansions of the thought expressed in the lead sentence, or they may continue the train of events suggested in the lead sentence. Some writers outline each paragraph before composing it. Some writers complete their piece and, if a paragraph seems clumsy and does not read well, will then outline it to help them reconstruct it. A paragraph may have a lead sentence which is not comprehensive enough or is too comprehensive. Such a lead sentence needs to be replaced by a new sentence. A paragraph may contain one or two sentences which belong in some other paragraph. Sometimes every sentence belongs in the paragraph but the sentences are not in a logical sequence. Here is a paragraph quoted from "A Seat Belt Could Save Your Life," but the sentences are not in the order in which they appeared in the author's published version.

While speeding at better than 300 miles an hour on the Bonneville Salt Flats in Utah, Donald Campbell's Bluebird II was hit by crosswinds. He arrived at the hospital at the same time as a woman whose car, going 45 miles an hour, had hit a soft shoulder on the road. Yet Campbell, held in place by his belt and shoulder harness, suffered only a hairline skull fracture as his head struck the cockpit. She broke her leg, pelvis and shoulder. His machine hurtled through the air for 300 yards, rolled over three times and slid for another 80 yards. Thus probably the most dramatic illustration of the value of safety harness was provided last September by the British racing driver, Donald Campbell.

The above paragraph does not read well. The reader can make it out by studying it and rereading it, but only with difficulty. The sentences in the paragraph are not in logical sequence. Suppose the author outlined his thoughts for this paragraph. He might have made the following outline:

1. Statement that there is dramatic illustration of value of belt (lead).
2. Campbell's accident.
3. His injuries with a seat belt.
4. Woman's accident.
5. Her injuries.

Following the above outline we get the following paragraph:

> Probably the most dramatic illustration of the value of safety harness was provided last September by the British racing driver, Donald Campbell. While speeding at better than 300 miles an hour on the Bonneville Salt Flats in Utah, his Bluebird II was hit by crosswinds. The machine hurtled through the air for 300 yards, rolled over three times and slid for another 80 yards. Yet Campbell, held in place by his belt and shoulder harness, suffered only a hairline skull fracture as his head struck the cockpit. He arrived at the hospital at the same time as a woman whose car, going 45 miles an hour, had hit a soft shoulder on the road. She broke her leg, pelvis and shoulder.

This paragraph, quoted as it appeared in the published version, has its sentences in a logical sequence and reads well, and the reader can understand it without difficulty. It is well organized.

A piece should not read clumsily because of needless changes in point of view. James Thurber in his book *The Years with Ross* quotes Ross, as follows, about a manuscript of Thurber's.

> The sentence at (a) differs in nature from sentence at (b). In the (a) sentence you are writing from the viewpoint of the Bloodgoods. In the (b) sentence you are the omnipotent author, knowing all about it. Seems to me wrong.

An author should have a good reason for a change in point of view, and a change should seldom if ever be made in the same paragraph. Likewise, an author should have a good reason for a change from past to present tense. Many manuscripts written by writers-in-training have continual changes in point of view or of tense which spoil the tone and effect for the reader.

Individual sentences should be clear to the reader without his having to think or check back. The sentence "The men wheeled the stones to the top of the hill where they stayed" lacks clarity. It is not clear whether "they" refers to men or stones. Sentences may lack clarity in their relation to each other. "Bob did not get on with his brother Jack. He did not argue. He was sullen." Here the reader does not know to whom the pronoun "he" refers.

Sentences may be confusing because a word used by the author as a noun can be read as a verb. The following sentence is an example: "To a soldier untrained in fighting, an enemy is a person to avoid."

The above sentence is grammatical English, but it should be reconstructed for clarity's sake. Despite the comma after the word "fighting" a reader may think a soldier is "fighting an enemy." Hence, the sentence must be read twice to be understood.

Authors often write sentences with excess verbiage, with words which can be eliminated without any loss of meaning or color. Many adjectives and some adverbs are in this category. The word "very" rarely adds anything, and the prose will be more incisive with the word eliminated. What is the difference between a very nice day and a nice day?

An unusual word may be the best word in a particular sentence. But such unusual words should not be used again in the next few pages. The word "adage" is an example. If this word is repeated within a page or two, its unusualness gives it too much emphasis in the reader's mind. The word sticks out as if it were printed in red, so that the reader's flow of thought is interrupted.

Often an author acquires a pet word which he uses over and over again, a writing mannerism. A copyeditor estimated that the author Edison Marshall used the word "implacable" 75 times in a 300-page manuscript. Some writers overuse a pet phrase, as, for example, "in the mind's eye." Many a writer-in-training fills his manuscript with the superfluous words "of course." The elimination of such word-mannerisms is easy, once it is pointed out to an author.

Sometimes a sentence must be recast in order to get rid

of a superfluous word. The word "little" should be watched. For example, the sentence "There is little to that argument!" Why not say "That argument is weak."? The first sentence has six words with a total of 27 letters. The second sentence, with 18 letters in four words, has the same meaning but is sharper.

Specific facts are more effective than general statements. "Fifty million buffalo roamed the plains of the old West" is more effective than the general statement "Millions of buffalo roamed the plains of the old West." However, if for truth's sake the specific must have the word "probably" or "maybe," the specific sentence becomes similar to an ineffective general sentence. "Probably fifty million buffalo roamed the plains of the old West" is equivalent to saying "I, the author, think there were as many as fifty million buffalo roaming the plains of the old West, but the number may have been less." Both of these statements are weak. An author should consider reconstructing any sentence that requires the word "probably." In the above, perhaps it would be better to use two or three sentences to make it clear that there were a lot of buffalo. Perhaps something like the following would be satisfactory:

> The plains of the old West contained an innumerable number of buffalo. So common, so ever present were they, that a camper became oblivious to their presence, just as someone camping in the New England woods today becomes oblivious to the ever present, ever numerous squirrels and birds.

Colorful expressions help the effectiveness of the writing if not used too often. Churchill in a speech said "There will be fighting in the Mediterranean and elsewhere before the leaves fall." "Before the leaves fall" is more colorful than "before autumn" or "before November." A colorful sentence should never be used at the expense of meaning. *Dux femina facti* can be translated very loosely as "There's a woman in the case." This is more colloquial and colorful than the accurate translation "A woman led the expedition," but the added color is at the sacrifice of meaning.

Variety of sentence structure improves the writing. The Bible has series of sentences each beginning with the word "the." No one can quarrel with the beauty of the language of the King James version of the Bible, but to the modern ear a series of consecutive sentences beginning with the word "the" becomes monotonous. Likewise, sentences beginning or ending with a conditional phrase or clause should be interspersed with ones that contain only one subject, one verb, and one object. This gives variety.

Too many short sentences rob writing of its natural rhythm. They are apt to result in the sort of thing a child in second grade might write. However, the writer-in-training is in more danger of getting himself involved in very long sentences. Here is a sentence from a first manuscript submitted to an agent:

> The catwhistle of the sawmill had already whirred and screamed out the end of another week of work, and the Saturday afternoon was thus wrenched from the mill, which for twenty-four years had slowly, but with calculated deliberation, gnawed away at one hundred thousand acres of virgin timber at the predetermined rate of one hundred thousand board feet of lumber per day, excepting Saturday afternoons and Sundays, which were given over to the subjugation of the Methodists and Baptists and the freedom of the heathen.

Here is the above sentence broken up into shorter sentences:

> By Saturday afternoon the catwhistle at the sawmill had whirred and screamed out the end of another week. Every week for twenty-four years the catwhistle had slowly gnawed away at one hundred thousand acres of lumber per day. The catwhistle was silent Saturday afternoons, and silent Sundays, these days being given over to the subjugation of the Methodists and Baptists and the freedom of the heathen.

Long sentences are often bad English. Aside from this, once a long sentence is broken up into short ones, the author can cut and improve. In the above three-sentence paragraph it is easy to see that the first sentence and the first part of the last sentence say the same thing. There is pointless repetition. Moreover, the last part of the last sentence is not relevant, and does not belong in the paragraph. Eliminating the last sentence in its entirety, we have remaining not distinguished English but at least two consecutive sentences that are understandable.

Finally we come to the problem of individual words. Attributed to Mark Twain is the statement that the difference between the right word and almost the right word is the difference between lightning and the lightning bug. But what is the right word? The word that most nearly portrays the author's meaning.

An example of the right word is the use of the word "female" in the Kipling quotation, "The female of the species is more deadly than the male." There are many ways that this thought could have been expressed. For example: "The woman is more deadly than the man" or "The female sex is more deadly than the male sex." But Kipling's phrasing, applying to animals and to human beings, is an effective use of words.

In considering what is the right word the author has to consider each word in relation to other words and in relation to common usage. Suppose a girl writing a letter was asked to whom she was writing. Suppose the girl replied, "I am writing to my female parent." The girl here would be using the words "female parent" as a circumlocution for the word "mother," and the girl's reply (unless it is considered funny from its oddity) is pointless and ineffective. But suppose a girl were on trial for murder; suppose, when she is on the witness stand, that the lawyer asks her if her mother is alive. Then let us suppose that the girl replies "I never had a mother; I only had a female parent." Here the word "female" in connection with the word "parent" has an impact to the reader.

How to write the English language is taught in every high

school and college. Hence there are a large number of books which deal with words, style, phrasing. Fowler's *Modern English Usage* (Oxford University Press) is the best-known book on the meaning, use, and abuse of many familiar words and phrases. Fowler is an effective advocate of the use of the simple Anglo-Saxon words. Here is what Fowler has to say under the heading *Formal Words:*

> There are a large number of words differing from each other in almost all respects, but having this point in common, that they are not the plain English for what is meant, not the form that the mind uses in its private debates to convey to itself what it is talking about, but translations of these into language that is held more suitable for public exhibition.

Here are some of Fowler's examples:

Accommodation	Room
Announce	Give out
Bear	Carry
Comestibles	Food
Dispatch	Send
Felicitate	Wish joy
Remark	Say
Valiant	Brave

What Fowler is trying to say is that simple writing is more effective than pretentious, and hence the simple or common word expresses meaning most effectively. We do not comment on a restaurant's *comestibles* but rather on its *food,* and we *say* the food is good rather than *remark* that it is. If the author is using dialogue trying to show a pretentious character, *comestibles* may be the right word. Likewise if the author is trying to be funny, *comestibles* may be the right word, but then the author must satisfy himself that he is being funny. The axiom here is: use a right word, and if either of two words seem right, use the simplest or the one in common use.

Active sentences are apt to be more effective than passive sentences. The Latin *Dux femina facti* would be translated literally "The leader of the expedition was a woman." A more forceful translation would be "A woman led the expedition." The Latin passive had force to the ancient Romans. The English passive has less force to us today. Of course the passive has its place in the language for variety and to de-emphasize something, but it is often wise for an author to stare at each passive sentence. Some of them should perhaps be changed to the active.

Here is a quotation from Charles Ferguson's *Say It with Words* (Alfred A. Knopf) about the importance of strong verbs:

> The effect of preoccupation with verbs may at first unnerve you. You shudder at the weakness of your everyday supply. Then verbs begin to steal your thoughts. You shape a sentence, not for its sense, but to crack a verb like a whip. All of which can vex you and make you wish you could ease back into ooze and forget verbs altogether. But preoccupation fades gradually into habit, leaving a lively and lingering interest. In the end you find that if you exercise verbs reasonably in reverie and conversation, you will be the more likely to trot them out unostentatiously when public occasion demands.
>
> Once you are awakened to verbs, both reading and listening can serve actually to improve your writing skill. You nod to verbs and tuck them away mentally to remind you when no one can teach you. Listen to the verbs in Lincoln's Gettysburg address ". . . our fathers brought forth on this continent a new nation, *conceived* in liberty, and *dedicated* to the proposition that all men are *created* equal. . . ." Here verbs beat time and mark the cadence as they do in many great passages of prose we love or remember.

Charming and interesting as the above is, nevertheless any and all books dealing with words can be of only limited help to the writer-in-training. Both the well-known Fowler (written in dictionary fashion) and the recent, not well-known

Ferguson (written as a brilliant series of essays) have limited practical value to the writer-in-training. The study of words can be a fascinating hobby just as the study of chess can be, but it is doubtful if indulging in a love of words helps the hobbyist to be a better writer. A large vocabulary is an advantage to an author. His command of a large number of words may not give him a wider choice of words for the written page, but the larger the author's vocabulary, the more precise becomes the meaning of the familiar Anglo-Saxon words. An author who knows the meaning of the word *troglodyte* does not have a new word that he is ever likely to use, but the words *cave man* or *hermit* may have a more precise meaning to him, as a result of his acquisition of the word *troglodyte*. A large vocabulary has a possible disadvantage (although the advantages certainly outweigh the disadvantages) in that the author may be tempted to overuse the less common words of Latin and Greek origin, and underuse the common Anglo-Saxon words.

Of all the books in a writer's library, Bartlett's *Familiar Quotations* is one of the most helpful. The help is not from the thoughts contained in these quotations. What is of value is the superb use of words to express the thought. The method of expression makes a quotation memorable.

A student at Oxford University in England had a Dean named Dr. Fell, and this student attained fame from the following rhyme:

> I do not love thee, Dr. Fell,
> The reason why I cannot tell.

If this student had studied under a Dr. Roe, his rhyme might have been:

> I do not love thee, Dr. Roe,
> The reason why I do not know.

Perhaps this Dr. Roe quotation would have become famous, but such is doubtful. The name *Fell* has an unpleasant connotation to many; it is a good name for a villain, and the word *tell* has in common parlance a double meaning. From the word *tell* we gather that the author does not know why he doesn't love Dr. Fell, and cannot tell. The study of the actual use of words in memorable quotations is probably of more value to the writer-in-training than studying about words in Fowler or Ferguson.

A dictionary is indispensable for every author. Writers differ as to their preference for dictionaries and no one dictionary can be labeled the best. Most writers have a small one to help them with spelling, and a larger one for the enumeration of the meaning of a word. The most renowned dictionary is the original edition of the Oxford Dictionary in eleven enormous volumes. This is the great dictionary for the word-hobbyist; the least useful to the professional writer. For example, in this dictionary the derivations, the various meanings, and the various uses, of the word *fall* are described in over fifteen thousand words of text. To read, not to add for the mind to absorb, the complete coverance of this one word is time-consuming and overwhelming to the working writer.

Many writers have on their desks *Roget's Thesaurus,* a book in dictionary form giving the synonyms of most commonly used words. *The New Roget's Thesaurus in Dictionary Form* is the best edition. Theoretically this book should help a writer's word imagination. Actually it seems of limited value. To anyone with writing experience words seem to flow. When a writer recognizes an inappropriate word in his copy, usually a better word comes to his mind. Some writers say that when they are tired, the right word comes to them less often, and use of the thesaurus improves their word selection. Maybe this is so, but most writers feel that the dictionary can serve the thesaurus' purpose and is of more value.

The ability to write good English, which means the ability to write clear English, is essential for the successful writer. Again, in *Say It with Words* Ferguson writes:

Only one who scans the learned journals or travels the conference circuit realizes how intense the cult of incomprehensibility has become in our time, and what kind of talk it was that led the late Maudy Maverick to mint the term *gobbledygook.* The term came after a committee meeting in Washington at which the chairman spoke at length about "malajustments co-extensive with problem areas . . . alternate but nevertheless meaningful minimae . . . utilization of factors which a dynamic democracy can be channelized into both quantitative and qualitative phases.

The English in the above is atrocious, incomprehensible, and inexcusable, but the trouble arises from bad thought or the lack of thought. Either the chairman had nothing of value to say or had not thought out what he had to say. Clear English requires clear thinking. With this neither dictionaries nor books discussing words can help. We come back to where we started in the first chapter, namely the theme-idea. If the theme-idea has been thought out and analyzed, if the material for the piece has been gathered and a good selection made, if the article has been organized via an outline, even if necessary to the outlining of individual paragraphs, adequate English will usually result. The organization of thoughts and the organization of words merge into one.

5

MARKETING THE ARTICLE

Once an author has developed a theme-idea and has done enough research to satisfy himself that there is sufficient material to write a satisfactory article, he should explore possible markets. He does this by submitting an outline or description of the proposed piece to magazine editors. What the author has may not be as suitable as he thinks. His theme-idea may not be worth building into an article. Only editorial reaction will give him the answer. Or the author's theme-idea may be good but there may be mechanical obstacles in the way of a sale. An editor may say no because he has a large inventory of purchased but unpublished pieces, and is not actively in the market. He may say no because he has previously purchased a piece on a similar subject. Or an editor, perhaps from personal whim, may not like the subject matter or the theme-idea for his subscribers. The editor of one of the popular magazines rejected a theme-idea for an article on snakes. He told the agent that he had more pregnant women among his subscribers than any other magazine in America.

Another reason for querying an editor in advance with an outline is that magazines differ in the way their articles are written and in their length requirements. The author needs to know in advance whether to tailor his article for *Reader's Digest,* or for *Look,* or for the New York *Times* Magazine Section. Finally, on the basis of an outline, an editor may make helpful comments to an author as to how a piece should be handled, and so enhance the likelihood of a sale.

If an editor will not approve an outline, he would be extremely unlikely to approve and purchase the finished piece, and an author should query someone else. If the writer finds no editor who will approve the outline, the project had better be dropped. A few writers skip the outline query stage. In the case of the humorous piece or the familiar essay, this may be wise. Something humorous must be humorous, and no editor can express an intelligent opinion from an outline as to how funny a piece will turn out to be. The familiar essay, so rarely published, should be almost a little work of art, and this cannot successfully be prejudged. With the great mass of article theme-ideas editors expect to be queried in advance through the medium of an outline.

A professional writer selects the magazine to be queried by studying the contents of many publications, and deciding upon a magazine that seems appropriate for his theme-idea. A magazine is a collection of short pieces, a package published at regular intervals. An editor is looking for good pieces of a particular type, those that fit into the magazine's editorial concept. No one familiar with *The New Yorker* or with *Reader's Digest* could mix up the magazines. Possibly one piece in one of those publications might be suitable for the other. Any six pieces from the *Digest* have the *Digest* ring; they fall into the *Digest* pattern and could not conceivably be in *The New Yorker*. *McCall's, The Ladies' Home Journal,* and *Good Housekeeping* have the women's-magazine concept. They differ little from each other (which may be one reason why they are not more successful financially). Most of the articles in any one of the women's magazines would fit into either of the other two women's magazines.

An editorial concept requires uniformity of types of subjects and types of theme-ideas, with the material presented not in a uniform manner but in a semiuniform manner. *Holiday* and *True* differ in the kind of theme-idea they would publish. *Holiday* and *National Geographic Magazine* do not differ much in their type of theme-idea, but they differ materially in the way their articles are handled. In some magazines there is uniformity even in the writing. It would not be difficult to imagine that one half of the pieces in an issue of *Reader's Digest* were written by the same author.

An author should decide for whom his theme-idea seems possible and whether it seems possible for him to handle the material and compose the writing so as to fit the magazine's editorial concept. The magazine selected should be queried. An intelligent query to a logical market impresses the editor of that market, and even if the response is negative, the way is paved for the next query.

Perhaps the theme-idea seems appropriate for any one of a dozen markets. In such a case beginning authors are often advised to start at the top, offering their outlines first to the highest paying market. If a negative answer is received, then to the next best market, etc. The author of this volume does not recommend this procedure. Most authors do not sell to *Reader's Digest* or to *McCall's* until after considerable publication in minor markets. Getting to the top by stages is recommended. Sell and get published in the minor markets and then try for better.

We have discussed in the previous chapter outlines prepared to help an author organize his material. Such an outline may be appropriate for an editor's eye, but often a new outline should be prepared.

An outline for editors should be from three to six paragraphs or not more than two typewritten pages. Usually one page is sufficient. The finished manuscript should be typed double-spaced to facilitate editing; an outline is usually single-spaced. It should contain the following:

1. The theme-idea plus a tentative title for the piece.
2. The way the piece will open.
3. A short resumé of the scope of the material.
4. The way the piece will end.
5. The approximate length of the piece.

6. A statement as to whether there are good anecdotes and, if not obvious, a statement as to the availability of material.

Sample paragraphs of what is to be in the finished piece should never be in the outline. No editor can judge a finished piece from sample paragraphs.

An author in his outline should take his work seriously, or at least pretend to. One experienced article writer ended his outline with the statement, "There will be more goodies to come." The editor rejected the query. When the agent inquired as to why a good theme-idea outlined by a very competent writer was rejected, the editor replied that the author was planning to write the piece with his tongue in his cheek, that the author obviously did not believe in what he was doing, and hence the result was likely to be unsatisfactory. In this case the agent went dashing over to see the editor, suggested that the reference to goodies was probably inserted after a couple of highballs, that the writer did take his work seriously, etc. The piece was written and purchased, but it was touch and go due to one silly sentence in the author's outline.

The outline should have a title, if for no other reason than to give it a name for the editor's record. A catchy title may help interest an editor in a theme-idea. An author proposed a piece on the horses which draw the Queen of England's coach. The author's title, "All the Queen's Horses," probably helped him obtain the assignment.

It is an unwritten rule that an editor can ignore the author's title and publish the article with the editor's invention of a title. Probably half of the published articles carry titles dreamed up by editors. Of course, editors' titles can be crazy, and the author can only keep a stiff upper lip. A piece on a restaurant in southern Alaska was published by a magazine under the title "Arctic Hotspot." The author received about a hundred letters from readers pointing out that the restaurant was six hundred miles south of the Arctic Circle and was not a hotspot. The editor who entitled this piece should have had his head examined.

The author should accompany the outline with a letter of transmittal, which may read as follows:

> Dear Mr. Editor:
>
> Enclosed is an outline of a proposed article on *Water Pollution*. Would you be interested to read an article by me based upon the outline?
>
> Very truly yours

If other magazines within the last couple of years have published pieces on the same subject, the author may want to give title, magazine, and date of publication of such pieces. The author wants to do this to show that he has done his homework. Also, he does not want an approval of his theme-idea to be reversed later on because other magazines have treated the subject. The author considers his theme-idea substantially different from the articles published by other magazines, but a *McCall's* editor, for example, may think the theme-idea too similar. If similarity is going to prevent a sale, the author wants to know in advance so as to save himself the labor of further research and writing.

An author who is peculiarly qualified to write a particular piece may want to say so in his letter of transmittal. However, being president of a garden club will not impress an editor as to an author's expertness with flowers; being a trained horticulturist may be in the author's favor. If an author proposes to write about a disaster in which he was physically involved, he may want to mention this fact. An author who has sold one or more articles recently to good markets may want to mention this as evidence of his proficiency. Minor publications, as for instance a small town paper, will not impress an editor and had better be left unsaid.

There should be no attempt at salesmanship in either the outline or in the letter of transmittal. An author should not say why he thinks an article on a particular subject will be effective or popular with the magazine's readers. It is the editor's function to judge that, and most editors do not like to be told how to conduct their business.

An author should not put in his letter of transmittal anything about the rights for sale or about the rights reserved or about copyright. Only amateurs do this. The rights sold to a magazine are the rights the magazine regularly buys, and the magazine takes care of copywriting its entire contents at the time of publication.

Likewise, an author should not enclose with his letter of transmittal copies of his published articles. At this stage the author is submitting for editorial approval a theme-idea and how he proposes to handle the material. Approval or disapproval of the writing will be rendered on the basis of the finished piece.

In general, the shorter the letter of transmittal the better. Editors are busy and are not impressed by long letters. If they want further information from the author, they will ask for it.

Some authors incorporate their outline in the letter of transmittal. For example:

> Dear Mr. Editor:
>
> I want to write an article on *Water Pollution* . . .

The rest of the letter is a carefully prepared outline ending with "very truly yours." This method is perfectly satisfactory to the editor. One objection from the author's point of view is that for each query a new letter outline has to be typed.

If the author has corresponded previously with a particular editor, that is the person to whom a letter of transmittal should be directed. When approaching a market for the first time, the author should not address the editor-in-chief. The top editor probably will not correspond with an author who has not sold to his magazine. The writer should examine the masthead of the magazine. If there is an article-editor designated, he should be queried. Otherwise pick at random one of the under-editors. The author is knocking at the door to get someone interested in him and in his theme-idea. An unimportant editor, interested, is valuable; an editor-in-chief, uninterested, is valueless.

Writers-in-training should not request an interview with an editor who has never published them. Such an attempt is likely to make the editor feel that he is being pestered or high-pressured. The editor wants to consider an outline in solitude. If he is favorably inclined, he wants to consult his colleagues and the editor-in-chief. An editor is not influenced because he knows or likes an author. The theme-idea and outline must sell itself.

After an author has sold one or more pieces to a magazine a personal interview is often helpful. The editor will be glad to see the author, and may have suggestions as to how to handle a piece, suggestions which will come forth more readily in conversation than in correspondence. Because of the pieces purchased, the editor has confidence in the writer's proficiency. The editor may suggest to the author the nucleus of an idea or even (though this is rare) a theme-idea.

Authors often want to submit copies of the same outline simultaneously to more than one magazine in order to get faster action. Considerations of outlines and rejections take time. However, this procedure is not recommended. If two magazines both express interest, the author will irritate the magazine he does not write for, and hurt himself for the future. Authors are apt to think of theme-ideas as very timely. Few are. Magazines are not newspapers and are not concentrating upon timeliness. The average article is not published until three months or more after acceptance.

Occasionally an author must have fast action. If an author wants to interview and write a profile of a celebrity who will be in New York City for a few days during the next week and then leave for Paris, time is of the essence. The best way for the author to handle this is by telephone. Call one editor after another, explain the hurry, and send the outline to the first really interested editor. Make the telephone conversations short.

How long a magazine takes to render an opinion about an outline depends upon the magazine, the individual editor, the standing of the writer, and other circumstances. *The Saturday Evening Post* is quick; *The Ladies' Home Journal,* slow. Some *Reader's Digest* editors are quick; some slow. *Esquire* is a tortoise. Rejections tend to be quicker than approvals. Perhaps the editor queried is quick but his colleagues are slow. After an editor has had an outline for two weeks, the author should write a very short, polite note asking the editor in question if he has reached a decision. In general, the more lowly the editor, the slower he is.

It is not necessary to enclose a stamped self-addressed envelope when submitting an outline, but doing so often encourages a quicker decision. An author should always keep a copy or carbon of his outline. He may receive an acceptance or rejection and not get back the outline.

When an author's outline is approved, he receives what is called an assignment. The editor says go ahead and makes a note of the theme-idea as a piece he expects to receive and purchase. He may even tentatively assign the piece to a particular forthcoming issue in his magazine.

On the basis of the assignment, the author completes his research and writes his piece. His letter of transmittal accompanying the completed piece should be short. It should remind the editor that he asked to see the piece. One reason for this is to remind the secretary or whoever first opens the envelope that this is a piece that the magazine is interested in. Occasionally the letter of transmittal may include,

1. Verification of a fact or facts. For example, if it is a proposed piece on a battle in the Second World War, and the author has a letter from a general in

command of the battle who makes statements at variance with most previous authorities, such letter may be enclosed.

2. A letter from some expert who has read the piece and vouches for the accuracy of the factual statements made. This should only be done in the case of a somewhat technical piece where the author would not be considered an authority. Never enclose a letter from a friend praising a piece or saying it is good. The editor will make his own judgment of that.

After reading the completed manuscript the editor may buy, the editor may ask for revision and then buy, or he may reject. Perhaps one fourth of assigned articles which are completed according to the outline do not work out and are rejected. Trouble usually arises from one of the following reasons:

1. The material promised in the outline is not there or is of such a nature as not to support the theme-idea. For example, suppose the outline proposes an article on plankton. Perhaps the facts do not point to the food possibilities suggested in the outline. Or maybe the author knew the limitation of the facts, but unconsciously has gilded the lily a bit in his outline in order to obtain an assignment. The experienced writer never exaggerates in his outline; the writer-in-training trying to sell himself sometimes does.
2. Occasionally an author receives an assignment and then bad luck strikes before the piece is completed. Perhaps a rival magazine publishes a piece on a somewhat similar theme-idea. Despite the assignment the potential buyer reneges because of the activity of a rival magazine, something beyond the control of the author. Sometimes the author discovers the forthcoming rival piece in the course of his live

research. In such case the author should consult his editor and probably abandon the piece, but often the author takes a chance. The two pieces may come out so differently as not to compete. The rival magazine may delay publication or never publish.

3. Likewise, a news event may knock out a piece. The attack on Pearl Harbor knocked out many an article assigned the week or two previously. A divorce or a scandal or death may make a proposed profile of an individual no longer desirable for publication.
4. A change of editors or a change of editorial policy may cause a magazine to no longer want to buy and publish an assigned piece.
5. An editor may think that a script is so bad that revision will not save it. Perhaps the author has just fallen down on the job, or perhaps he suggested a theme-idea which was not a happy one for him to handle. Some authors can write one type of article very well, and some other type not so well. Of course, when an editor thinks an article is poor, he may be wrong in his judgment. How good or bad an article is, is a matter of opinion.

The dream of an article writer is to have an editor propose a theme-idea, agree to pay a large price for it upon delivery, and agree to publish the completed piece exactly as written. Such dreams are out of this world.

In nine cases out of ten the author has to find and develop his own theme-idea. The writer-in-training has to spend a great deal of time and, often, some money for expenses, with the question of a sale and payment being a matter of speculation. The professional writer with many sales under his belt is relieved of much of the risk, but he will run into troubles all his writing life. He can seldom completely remove the risk of no sale and, hence, of time wasted.

Many authors are tempted to submit to editors first or rough drafts of their articles. They want to do this partly in the hope that an editor will help them revise or rewrite the piece, partly for encouragement. Doing this is always a mistake. Editors are not instructors in writing, and if they can help, their help will be much greater on a finished piece, the author's best work, than in the case of an unfinished, half-good piece. An author should get encouragement from his family. A manuscript should be written, rewritten, and completed to the author's satisfaction before an editor sees it. It can be stated as an absolute rule: never submit a first draft.

Editors often express willingness to read first drafts or even ask to see them. They do this partly to please the author, and partly to insure their getting first look. They want to get their clutches on something which may be good before one of their competitors gets it. An editor may have something to gain from reading a first draft; an author has much to lose. Many a sale has been lost because of submitting a half-good manuscript. No author should ever show his wares until he is satisfied with his material, his organization, and his writing.

There are certain mechanical directions which should be followed by all authors when submitting their completed pieces. A manuscript should be cleanly typed, double-spaced on fairly heavy white paper, with wide margins, and with a minimum of handwritten corrections. If a manuscript is worth writing, it is worthwhile making it as easy as possible for the editor to read. Number the pages consecutively. There should be a title and the author's name and address on the title page or on the first page. There is no need for the title or the author's name to be on every page. It is not customary for an author to personally sign his name at the end of the piece.

The words in a manuscript should be correctly spelled. Incorrect spelling is sloppy, and the editor may wonder if the author isn't sloppy in other respects. Punctuation is different. Here there is little unanimity. *The New Yorker* exudes commas. *Reader's Digest* eschews them. No author should cultivate eccentricity but otherwise punctuate as the spirit moves.

An author should not staple together the pages of a manuscript or staple on a cover or folder. No editor wants to exert physical labor to keep a manuscript open while reading. Also, an editor may read a few pages and then be interrupted, and he does not want the manuscript to shut so that later on he has to hunt for his place. An article should be held together with a paper clip, should not be folded, but mailed in a large envelope. If desired, a piece of cardboard can be inserted in the envelope to keep the manuscript from getting creased.

When submitting a manuscript, enclose a self-addressed, stamped envelope for the return of the piece. Retain a carbon. Manuscripts occasionally get lost in the mail. Magazine publishers have been known to lose or misplace a manuscript or individual pages, although this occurs very rarely. Another reason for retaining a copy is that editors, in the case of a purchase, often ask for cutting or revision. If they are buying and paying for the piece, they may want to retain the physical manuscript. In such a case the author revises from his carbon. Sometimes an editor may telephone about a particular statement in a piece. The author needs a copy for reference.

The mass circulation magazines will usually send their own photographer to take pictures after the piece has been purchased. Photographs supplied by the author will not increase the chances of a sale. The exception is an important photograph, perhaps an old one which the magazine photographer would find difficult to obtain.

Minor publications often expect the author to obtain photographs, and sometimes will only consider a manuscript that is accompanied by photographs. Any photographs submitted should be interesting ones that will reproduce satisfactorily. The author needn't be a camera fiend, but he should learn enough to recognize professional photography.

When a manuscript is submitted to one of the large circulation magazines, an under-editor will first read the piece. He will then obtain one or more readings from other under-editors. If the comments are unfavorable, and no revision seems possible, the piece will be returned. If the piece seems at all possible, it will be given to the top editor, the editor-in-chief, for decision. If the decision is negative, the under-editor will then return the piece with a letter of much regret. If the decision is favorable, the under-editor will then write or telephone the author offering to buy, and suggesting a price. Sometimes the under-editor will return the piece with the request that the author revise and resubmit. If this occurs, acceptance of the revised piece is probable.

A magazine may make its decision in two or three days or in several weeks. After an article has been in an editorial office for two weeks, there is no harm in the author's writing a short note requesting a decision. Editorial delay is the great exasperation of the writing trade. When DeWitt Wallace, owner and editor of *Reader's Digest,* was reproved over the *Digest's* slowness in rendering decisions, he wrote an agent as follows:

> Dear ——,
>
> You remember the quotation of Lord Mansfield. "Make your decisions quickly. Never give your reason for your decision. Your decisions may be right; your reason is sure to be wrong."
>
> Yours sincerely,
> Wally

Before a purchased manuscript is sent to the printer, it is copyedited. This means that an under-editor or copyeditor corrects typographical errors and checks on spelling. Punctuation and capitalization are made to conform to the rules of the magazine. Usually there is some minor elimination or rearrangement of words for the improvement of syntax.

Aside from this there is usually some cutting in the sense of shortening the article. Editors cut partly to improve the manuscript (most authors tend to overwrite), partly to keep their articles short. Most magazines prefer to offer their readers twelve short pieces, for example, rather than eight long ones. Also, articles are cut to make space for advertisements received at the last moment or, perhaps, so that the article will stop at the bottom of a page. Cutting often improves the readability of the piece. With last-minute cutting, it may be seriously impaired.

With the exception of an occasional connective word or sentence, no editor of a national magazine will write anything into a piece without consulting the author in advance. Inserting into a piece words or ideas which the author has not written or approved would be a major editorial crime. Even the minor markets are rarely guilty of this. Some magazines will send an author proofs. Time permitting, most will upon request. The author can then correct the cut version. Even if this is done, however, there may be further last-minute cutting.

6

INCOME OF THE ARTICLE WRITER

A writer may be someone who scribbles a lot but fails to publish, or a writer may be a housewife or a newspaper reporter who averages a published piece a year. There are people who perhaps sell a piece to *Reader's Digest* and then, five years later, sell a piece to *Look* magazine—people who write only when they have unusual material from some extraordinary personal experience. There are people who have a part- or full-time job but regularly and assiduously devote time to writing, with appreciable success. Their income from their pen may be anywhere from one fifth to one half of their total income. Such people may write almost exclusively for the minor markets, or write regularly for the major markets with only a couple of sales a year. Then there are ins-and-outers, people who write successfully for a year or two and then abandon the occupation. Finally, there are the full-time writers whose principal income is from their pen.

There is no way of estimating the total number of writers, partly because of the lack of definition of who is a writer, and partly because of the fluid nature of any categories of writers. The Society of Magazine Writers, an organization of successful professional non-fiction writers, primarily in the article field, has a membership of about two hundred. Perhaps there are another two hundred writers who are not members. These four hundred writers are free-lance, their own boss. They submit outlines and articles which may or may not be purchased.

Perhaps one half of these four hundred writers are full-time workers; one half, part-time. The part-time writers produce and sell consistently and add appreciably to their income. Each year some of these part-time writers move into the full-time category, and some of the full-time writers move into the part-time.

The incomes of these four hundred writers range from $5000 to $50,000 a year, with individual incomes varying from year to year. Probably four fifths of them make less than $15,000 a year. At least one fifth of these writers earn a substantial part of their income from books or from some writing medium other than article writing. The more successful the writer is, the more likely it is that a substantial source of his income is from books.

There are, in addition to the above four hundred, some fifty staff writers hired by the high-paying magazines to write articles on assignment. These staff writers may be entirely on salary, or they may have an office at the magazine, use the magazine's stationery, but be paid only as the magazine uses their material. In most cases they write only for the magazine which employs them. Many of the theme-ideas for their pieces are dreamed up by the editors. Their salaries or drawing accounts run from $5000 to $25,000, but their total income is often much larger. Staff writers may resign and move into the free-lance field, and free-lancers may become staff writers. Many editors are former staff writers.

The minimum rates of the top markets for a full-length article are from $750 to $1000. A successful article writer can fairly quickly increase his rate to $1500 per article. He finds it difficult to obtain any more. As it is rare for an article writer to be able to sell more than six pieces a year to the top markets, his income is small. There may be additional income from two or three sales to minor markets and a little dribbling income from reprints of published pieces, but his total income is probably under $12,000. Sometimes he can increase his income by becoming prolific. Usually an increased income depends upon a higher basic stipend for each article sold or extra money from another writing medium.

A writer much in demand may receive half payment or even full payment for a completed article which the editor does not like and is not going to publish. The magazine may have contracted for the piece—that is to say, the author agreed to write it as per his outline, and the magazine agreed to pay for it upon delivery willy-nilly. Or the magazine may pay for it without being legally obligated, just to keep a well-known author happy and willing to write further pieces for them. However, no author likes to deliver an unacceptable piece. He misses the reward of publication, and if this situation happens more than once, the magazine will offer no further contracts and no further payments for unacceptable pieces. An author, no matter how successful in the past, must continue to satisfy his markets or he will lose them.

Some magazines, notably *Reader's Digest,* will make what is called a commitment. They will approve an author's outline and agree to pay $250 to $300 if the piece is rejected, and the author's normal price if the piece is accepted. It is doubtful if the *Digest* purchases one half of the pieces on which they make a commitment.

Magazines are edited by human beings with the eccentricities of human beings. A few years ago the *Digest* editorial minds decided they wanted an article on the art of walking. A theme-idea and outline was duly approved and a 5000-word piece completed and offered to the magazine. This magazine sometimes prints articles as original pieces, sometimes lets other magazines print them, the *Digest* then reprinting. The *Digest* editor said that he would buy the piece on walking, provided the *Atlantic Monthly* first bought and published it. The *Digest* could then reprint from the *Atlantic.* The agent suggested *Harper's Magazine.* The editor said no, he would only buy it if the piece first received the accolade of the *Atlantic Monthly.* The agent offered the manuscript to the *Atlantic,* which promptly returned it. It was then suggested to the *Atlantic* editor that a mere one thousand words on the art of walking would not wreck the magazine.

The *Atlantic* agreed to cut the piece and paid $150 for a thousand words on the art of walking. This $150 was forwarded to the *Digest*. The *Digest* then paid the agent, in behalf of the author, $1000. However, it is a house rule that every piece printed in the *Digest* must be shorter than the length of the piece first published in another magazine. After all, it is a *digest* magazine. As a cut version of a 1000-word cut version on the art of walking is unlikely to have much substance, the *Digest* never published the piece.

How much a writer can obtain for his articles depends partly upon how ingenious he is with theme-ideas; partly upon his ability to always produce a first-class completed script. Perhaps twenty of the most successful practitioners obtain $4000 an article from their best markets; in a few cases, where the material is exclusive and exciting, even more. Usually these successful writers have latched on to one magazine, *The New Yorker*, or *Life*, or *Reader's Digest*, almost as staff writers. Although they originate their own theme-ideas and operate on a free-lance basis, one magazine has first chance at their material and publishes most of it. Another possibility of making a great deal of money, $20,000 to $100,000 is by writing a book which is serialized in a magazine. Possibilities of the non-fiction book will be discussed in a later chapter.

This volume has tried to make it clear that the actual composing of the words of a manuscript is only part of a writer's work. A professional writer is a combination of idea man, researcher, outliner, writer, reviser, and correspondent. The profession of preparing and selling articles is a varied and arduous occupation. Its time requirements are perhaps two sixths theme-idea developing and research work, one sixth organizing, one sixth writing, one sixth revising, and one sixth corresponding.

Many authors use the first couple of hours of each working day in actual composition. This is the time they are freshest. Next they do research work. Then some work at notes, outlines, or revising. Perhaps the end of the day is devoted to correspondence and general reading. A writer's correspondence is considerable. He is continually trying to obtain some out-of-print book or the back issue of a magazine, continually writing to experts, trying to check a fact or obtain an opinion, continually writing for appointments or writing letters of transmittal to editors.

In all walks of life people differ in their speed of accomplishment, in the amount of work they can accomplish in a day. Of course, writers differ in this respect, but success does not necessarily favor the rapid composer. Perhaps two to five pages in four hours would be common, but there are writers much slower than this and there are writers who will finish a piece of fifteen or twenty pages in a sitting. A successful writer does not have to accelerate his actual composition, but it is very important for him to get his other work done expeditiously. He must crowd as much live and library research as possible into one day, get his notes and outlines organized in a minimum of time, and not dawdle over his correspondence. Finally, a writer must always make time for the reading of what other writers in his field are producing, and what his markets are publishing.

A writer's life is beset with the frustration of delay. An appointment is broken which delays a writer's live research; an essential book from a state library arrives late, or an editor takes an unconscionable time in considering an outline, compounding the delay. The method of beating these inevitable delays is for the writer to keep several projects going simultaneously. Every week the professional is searching for new theme-ideas, doing research, outlining, and writing on more than one subject.

There is also the frustration of much work that never comes to fruition. A theme-idea may blow up after it has been researched; the facts do not support it. Or an outline may be prepared and no editor may like it. Some completed articles, despite an assignment based upon an outline, will not be purchased. However, many professionals claim that the work done on unsuccessful theme-ideas or the work on pieces which do not sell is work not completely wasted. They claim that everything is grist to their mill and that at least part of what is worthless today can be used tomorrow.

There are authors whose desks seem one inch high with papers, yet who know exactly where each research note is when they want it. However, a large number of authors organize elaborate folders, prepare different ones for different phases of their research on one article, and further ones for outlines and first drafts. Often a writer scribbles notes to himself in a pocket notebook, and at the end of the day tears off the pages and inserts them in the appropriate folders. In order to avoid needless typing, many authors, in revising their copy, make use of shears and a stapler. A paragraph saved from a revised or discarded page will be cut out and stapled into its proper place in the new draft.

Reference books most used by a writer must be handy. Edison Marshall has built himself a turnstyle, or large wooden Lazy Susan, which stands beside his desk holding the *Encyclopedia Britannica*. The books are in groups of four with the spines facing the ceiling. Edison Marshall can rotate the Lazy Susan, pick out the volume he needs, look up the reference, and return the book to its place with a minimum of time and effort.

The average writer who works from his home has great advantages over the business man. A writer's time is his own, and he loses none traveling back and forth to his work. Lunching at home is cheaper and better than in the average restaurant. He has certain tax savings, such as taking off part of his rent or house expense as a business expense (his office). His problem is to get his family to consider his job as continuous work, never interrupt him, leave him absolutely alone. Recently a writer said to the author of this volume, "Mr. Reynolds, I am a honeydew." I said, "You are what?" The writer continued, "Yes, I am a honeydew, I cannot work at home. You see, my wife says 'Honey, do this, and Honey, do that,' and I cannot work at home." This silly story illustrates one of a writer's frustrations; he cannot do his work effectively if he is constantly interrupted to go out and get the mail or let out the dog or turn the mattress, etc.

Many fiction writers, in order to avoid interruption, work at night, perhaps from 9:00 P.M. to 3 or 4 in the morning. Because most research work must be done in the daytime, such hours are not very practical for the non-fiction writer. Some authors hire a one-room office and commute to work. Many fix up an old barn or shed as an office, such being far enough away from their home so that they do not hear the telephone.

Some writers try to conserve their time by hiring a researcher for their library research. This may be helpful with a book-length project, especially one based primarily on library research. A researcher seldom helps an article writer. A writer must himself read his material so as to make his own selection of what he will use. The researcher can only cull out the material, saving the writer from having to read what is not apropos. The time involved in conferences with the researcher usually exceeds the time saved by the researcher.

Some writers employ a secretary for their correspondence and for typing versions of their manuscripts. This again rarely saves time. A person fast on the typewriter can rush out a dozen letters almost as fast as he can dictate them, read them, correct them, and sign them. The outside typing of various drafts of an article seldom saves time, because most writers revise each draft as they copy.

However, a large number of writers do have the final version of their manuscript typed by a professional typist. It is desirable to have the final product almost letter perfect, and many an author finds the final preparation of his manuscript arduous and time-consuming. Some writers' wives undertake this function.

Most writers peck away at their typewriters with two

fingers and usually obtain a speed comparable to a secretary who has learned the touch system. Writers who have worked on a newspaper often type their first drafts. Others will transcribe one or more pages in longhand; then copy (simultaneously revising) on the typewriter; then cut, write in, expand, with pencil; and, finally, recopy with further revisions on the typewriter. A handful of elderly writers who did not grow up in the typewriter age do everything in longhand.

Most people in their working hours see and talk with people engaged in their own line of work. Writing is a lone-wolf occupation. Some writers long to talk shop with other writers. These are the ones who attend writers' conferences or meetings of The Author's Guild or the Society of Magazine Writers. A substantial number of writers seem to prefer never to meet anyone else in their profession.

A fiction writer can live anywhere in the world without being under any handicap. A certain number have never been to New York City and have never met their publishers or agents. For an article writer there are distinct advantages in living in the vicinity of New York, close to their markets. It is not essential but very helpful to be able to discuss theme-ideas and outlines with editors. Also, New York City, the headquarters of so much in America, is perhaps the best place for live research. Most celebrities, when they visit the city, are available for interviews; many businesses, unions, and other organizations have some tie to New York. Politically, of course, Washington, D.C., is the center, but Washington is only an hour or so away from New York by plane. Article writers who live away from New York usually find it advisable to visit the city as often as five or six times a year.

PART II

7

HOW TO WRITE THE GENERAL NON-FICTION BOOK

This chapter will discuss the writing of general non-fiction books. These are books sold in bookstores or on newsstands in hard or soft covers. These are the type of books that may appear on non-fiction best-seller lists. Specialized books such as textbooks, travel guidebooks, medical books, reference books, juveniles, etc. will be excluded.

The author's first problem is to obtain an idea suitable for a long piece of work. Such an idea we shall call a book-idea. Theoretically, an author should be able to obtain a book-idea through the process outlined for an article, namely finding the nucleus of an idea and developing it into a full-fledged book-idea. Then the author should be able to develop through the same process several other book-ideas, and from these select the one that seems most promising. Some prolific professional writers find these procedures practical. However, most writers, especially in the case of their first long manuscript, do not do this.

What actually happens is that the author obtains somewhere a book-idea that appeals to him. This book-idea grows in his mind. He is driven forward. He cannot look for or consider other book-ideas until the one he is obsessed with becomes a book-length manuscript.

Every author should evaluate his book-idea before he is so involved psychologically that he cannot abandon his project. A compulsion to write, based upon a good book-idea, is a large factor in success. A compulsion to write, based upon a poor book-idea, means almost certain failure.

A good book-idea suggests a book that will meet three mechanical requirements.

The first requirement is length. Most non-fiction books should run to 60,000 words minimum, 200 typed pages. The manuscript can run much longer. *The Rise and Fall of the Third Reich* comprised over 500,000 words, about the maximum length practicable for publication in one volume.

Writers-in-training must not be led astray by what they may occasionally see in the physical form of a book. The fact that an article is printed and bound so that it looks like a book does not mean that it meets the qualifications of a book; it still remains an article. There are some semi-legitimate non-fiction books of short length such as the illustrated humorous book. These exceptions are few. Nearly every good book-idea calls for at least 60,000 words, and the writer-in-training had better plan on 80,000 words or more.

Many magazine theme-ideas are unsuitable for a book because there is not enough material for 60,000 words. How could an author write 60,000 words around the theme-idea of *A Seat Belt Could Save Your Life?* Writers-in-training sometimes complete a book project in 25,000–30,000 words. They have covered the subject. There was not enough important or interesting material related to the book idea for a 60,000-word manuscript. In such a case the author usually does not have a book. He has nothing.

The second mechanical requirement is unity. Instinctively a magazine writer knows that an article must have unity. With 60,000 or more words, and the resulting temptation to wander into bypaths, many a writer-in-training forgets the requirement. A book has unity when it is about one subject or several truly related subjects. A book on the problems of writing fiction and non-fiction would lack true unity. The problems of creative writing and feature writing are too different. A book on article writing and non-fiction books has unity because the two fields are related and one leads into the other. The biography of a man has unity. A haphazard collection of short biographies would not have unity. A collection of biographies of United States Senators and statesmen who have exhibited unusual courage, such as President Kennedy's *Profiles in Courage,* has unity. A book for housewives on how to be a good housekeeper would lack unity if it included recipes. Recipes belong in a cookbook.

The third mechanical requirement, really a part of unity, is a beginning and an ending. Some successful books lack these; every book is better if it can have them. Dana's *Two Years Before the Mast* starts on the day Dana sailed out of Boston harbor and ends two years later when the returning ship reached home. Often the beginning and the ending of a book cannot be determined until the material has been assembled, but it is desirable to have a book-idea which lends itself to a beginning and an ending. A manuscript which might have started earlier or later, a manuscript which might have continued but just stops, rarely make good books.

General non-fiction books may be divided into five categories, depending upon the book's primary purpose. These primary-purpose categories are:

Primary purpose to inform
Primary purpose to interest and entertain
Primary purpose to arouse emotion
Primary purpose to teach
Primary purpose to persuade

A good book-idea presupposes a book in one of these five categories. Some book-ideas handled one way will produce a book for one category; handled differently, they will fit into another category. For instance, a book on the building of the Panama Canal may be written as a serious account of a great American engineering achievement. It will then fit into the primary-purpose-to-inform category. However, the author may not be enamored of serious history. There may be a mass of curious facts and incidents around the men who built the Canal, so that a book could be written whose primary purpose is to interest and entertain.

The problems presented to the author depend upon the book's category. The author should consider what his completed manuscript will be like, into what category it will fit, and then determine whether he can solve the problems of the particular category.

Primary Purpose to Inform

Here the chief purpose is to give the reader information he wants to know or should know. Examples are history or serious biography.

Books in this category must be on an important subject. History is usually important, but the history of one obscure Indian tribe may be unimportant. The biography of a famous man is important enough for a book. A very minor historical figure may not be sufficiently important.

Some good theme-ideas for magazine articles are not important enough to justify a book. The Battle of Atlanta is perhaps an example. Gettysburg, the turning point in the Civil War, is important enough for a book. Chancellorsville, displaying Lee's military strategy, is probably important enough, but it is doubtful if the Battle of Atlanta was a significant enough battle to justify 60,000 words.

Primary Purpose to Interest and Entertain

Many popular non-fiction books are in this category. Although these books give the reader much information, their primary purpose is to interest and entertain. Often the interest results from the recounting of trivial but curious facts and incidents.

The writer of the interest-and-entertainment-purpose book should ask himself:

> Are there a large number of curious facts and incidents pertaining to the book-idea which will intrigue the reader?

A book on worms probably would not have enough such information. A book on ants or on bees would offer more possibilities. A book on all underground animals, worms, grubs, moles, might offer enough possibilities. In *A Night to Remember,* a book on the sinking of the *Titanic,* the following suggest possibilities for many curious facts and incidents:

> There were many well-known names like Vanderbilt on board.
> Some people were brave; some were cowardly.
> Different types of people were involved: first class, steerage, crew, officers, etc.
> There were variations of locale: *Titanic,* lifeboats, sea, rescue ships, etc.

The second question the writer of the interest-entertainment-purpose book should ask himself is:

> Does the book idea presuppose a book that will give the reader a feeling of progress? Will the reader want to keep reading?

A reader reads an information-purpose book to learn. A feeling of progress is unnecessary. But even in this category there is a quiet sense of movement just from the accumulation of information. The interest-entertainment-purpose book must have a framework which will give the reader a sense of progress. The reader must want to know what is going to happen next. Obtaining this is partly a matter of organization, which will be discussed later. However, the question is partly one of the nature of the material. A catastrophe book obviously will exhibit progress. The *Titantic* in *A Night to Remember* hits an iceberg, and the book continues until the last survivor is rescued. The entire account is one of progress. An interest-entertainment-purpose book on bees would be more difficult. Can such a book follow the life of a hive, or the history of man's obtaining honey from bees so that a feeling of progress exists? An essay-like book on bees would be difficult to write so as to hold the general reader's attention through 60,000 words. It would lack a sense of progress.

Primary Purpose to Arouse Emotion

An example of this type of book would be *Death Be Not Proud* by John Gunther. This is an account of the last years of a talented and attractive teen-age boy stricken with cancer and with no possibility of recovering. *Angel Unaware* by Dale Evans is another example. This is a book describing how the author loved and brought up a retarded, almost idiot, child. It is permeated with religious feelings. The writer of a book in this category should ask himself the following questions:

1. Can the emotion be so varied within the framework of the book-idea so that the reader will not get bored?
2. Can the over-all emotion be sustained through 60,000 words or more?

Often the answer to the second question is whether the tempo of the emotion can be increased as the book proceeds.

This category requires much creativity. It is the non-fiction category closest to fiction, and hence difficult for the teacher to make helpful suggestions. Unless the writer-in-training has published a considerable number of articles in this area, he should not attempt an emotion-purpose book.

Primary Purpose to Teach

With a book-idea that points to this category, the writer should ask himself:

1. Are there enough facts, methods, explanations to be said about the subject to warrant a book?

There might be an article on how to tie knots, but obviously there is not enough to be said to make a book. How the average man can fix household gadgets may be in the same category. Possibly such a book could be successfully written if every conceivable gadget were discussed, but this might involve discussing many obscure gadgets unknown to the average man, and hence the project would be getting away from the book-idea.

2. Have you, the author, new shortcuts to learning?

The author's book must help the student learn more rapidly than he would without the book. Has the author new methods not commonly known so that there is a need for his book?

3. Are there a lot of people who want to be taught the subject in question?

Obviously there are many people who want to learn how to play bridge or chess, but one should question whether there are enough people who want to know how to play cribbage so as to justify a cribbage book.

Primary Purpose to Persuade

Here the object is to persuade the reader that something is true or to urge him on to a particular course of action. Most, but not all, of the books in this category are publicity or propaganda books. These books will be discussed in the next chapter.

A good book-idea suggests a book with not only a primary purpose but with one or more secondary purposes. A purpose-to-inform book has some entertainment value, some anecdotes, and it may have powerful paragraphs to arouse the reader. These are secondary purposes. A purpose-to-interest-and-entertain book may have some information of importance in it, and often much information that is trivial. A purpose-to-teach book is not one hundred percent teaching.

The writer must weigh in his mind to what extent his book will have secondary purposes. How much entertainment value in a primarily informative book? Can the author sustain the emotion when writing a brutal assault on the feelings? Should he mingle his emotion with secondary purposes?

Essential to the evaluation of a book-idea is preliminary reading.

1. The author should read most of the books and any magazine articles which bear directly on his book-idea. If a biography is planned, all the previously published biographies on the figure should be read. If a catastrophe, magazine articles, newspaper accounts, and a book (if such exists) dealing with the catastrophe.
2. The author should do general reading, perhaps half a dozen books, in the area of interest. In the case of biography, histories of the period and biographies of contemporaries of his proposed figure. If a catastrophe, such as the attack on Pearl Harbor, books on the Hawaiian Islands and on the armed forces in the Pacific just before the Second World War.

On the basis of such reading the author should ask himself: Is there a place for my proposed book? If there is no previous book published on the subject, is a book warranted? If there are other books on the subject, what reason is there for the author to believe that he can produce a superior one? If the author's book-idea is in the information field, has he a new conception? Has he information previously unpublished, and hence unused by previous writers? William Shirer says in his introduction that he would not have attempted *The Rise and Fall of the Third Reich* had there not been available to him tons of German documents (diaries, letters, etc.) to which previous writers on Hitler and the Third Reich did not have access.

If the author's book-idea is in the interest-and-entertainment area, where is the reserve of entertaining material that the author can lay his hands upon so as to permit his book to be equal if not superior to similar books? If the author's proposal is a how-to-do-it book, how qualified is the author? If the book-idea is for an emotional book, has the author the basis for such, as Gunther did in *Death Be Not Proud?* Gunther was writing about his own son dying of cancer. It is not necessary to write about a member of one's family. It is necessary to have moving material. Perhaps the experiences of some friend or of a notorious murderer moved the author, and he feels that he can produce a book which will move the reader.

In examining other books, writers are faced with two dangers:

> 1. Many writers-in-training have a tendency to downgrade what has been published. This is the danger of overemphasizing what is bad about a book or what one does not like. The helpful attitude is to search for the excellence. There are some nuggets of gold in every book. The writer-in-training should search for these and then consider in what ways he could do even better.
> 2. Many a writer-in-training reads previous best sellers, and says to himself, "My first book probably won't be a best seller, my book does not have to be as good as the ones I have read." This point of view is unfortunate. No one can guarantee best sellers; the whims of popular taste will be discussed in a later chapter. Every writer is in competition with every other. The new writer must do as well as the name writer. If the writer-in-train-

ing does not conceive that his book will be as good as any comparable best seller, there is something wrong with his book-idea.

Organizing the Book

Let us assume that the writer-in-training, after preliminary research and much inward questioning, has definitely selected his book-idea. He is ready to start the organization.

The writer first prepares a description or outline of his book-idea. The outline designates a beginning, a main body of material, and an ending, and it places the book in one of the purpose categories. Next, the writer prepares chapter headings or tentative descriptions of the material proposed for each chapter.

The series of chapters must follow a pattern. The material in the chapters must coincide with the overall organization, an organization which would be there if the book was not broken up into chapters. Even a cookbook is not just a helter-skelter collection of chapters, each chapter containing a helter-skelter list of recipes. The chapters follow a pattern, perhaps from the simplest recipes to the most difficult, or perhaps from soup to dessert, or perhaps the pattern evolves from the nature of the ingredients called for in the recipes.

From the chapter headings the writer looks for the theme of each chapter. Just as an article has a theme, so a chapter has a theme. If a book has only one theme, this theme becomes the theme of every chapter. Often a book has several themes. In such a case an individual theme may be limited to one chapter or it may run through several chapters. Each new theme, whether it starts with Chapter Two or with Chapter Five, grows out of the previous theme so that the book has an inherent unity.

Suppose the book-idea is a biography. Perhaps the first chapter is the boyhood life of the author's subject. Was the boy a child genius or a poor student? Was he a scared rabbit of a kid or a devil-may-care kid always in revolt against his parents and school? Or perhaps the theme is that the boy was as normal as blueberry pie. The theme of the second chapter may be the rising ambition of the boy as he enters manhood, or perhaps this ambition theme is not reached until the third chapter.

If the author has a theme-idea for a disaster book, perhaps the first chapter deals with premonitions of trouble, or perhaps its theme is the slovenliness and laziness of the actors before the disaster struck. The theme of the second chapter may be the energy and courage of people who previously seemed useless.

Once an author gets chapter headings or short outlines of each chapter on paper, he should re-examine his whole project. It is usually necessary to revise the main outline and change some individual chapter outlines. The author is undertaking a mixed process. He is building his main outline from his chapter outlines and he is revising his chapter outlines to conform to his main outline.

Most biographies are told in a general chronological fashion, which gives a relatively simple organization to the book. However, there are usually minor complications because biographies are seldom completely chronological. One chapter may concentrate on the subject's campaign to be nominated and elected President of the United States. Another chapter, dealing with the subject's family relations, may flash back to the campaign year or before.

The outline for the interest-entertainment book may be extremely complicated. Here the author should work out a mosaic which determines the order of the chapters, and which runs through the material in the chapters. Suppose the author is writing an information book on how the Panama Canal was built. The author has four major types of problems that the builders of the Canal had to overcome:

1. The engineering problems.

   Sixty years ago these seemed overwhelming. Perhaps the blueprints had to be revised or discarded for new ones during the actual construction.

2. The medical problems.

   Men had to dig and they had to be kept alive, free from malaria and other diseases while living under most primitive conditions.

3. The national and international problems.

   France was involved. Panama had to be set up as an independent nation. The U. S. Senate had to settle the Canal tolls.

4. The internal political problems.

   Some of the American leaders were in disagreement and fighting among themselves.

The writer could divide his book into four separate parts as above. If he does he may run into repetition. The same event may have a bearing on more than one part, and it must be discussed wherever it has a bearing. A sense of progress may disappear from the book because each part must cover the same period of years. The author is in danger of ending up with four short books bound together under the pretense that they are one book.

Probably the writer will feel that he must weave the four threads of interest listed above into a tapestry. Each thread will cover much or all of the book, each one will influence the others. In *A Night to Remember* the author has to follow the activities of the captain, the engineers, the crew, the first-class passengers, and the steerage passengers, not to mention rescue ships, etc. *Wyoming Summer* by Mary O'Hara is an account of one summer when the author and her husband ran a riding camp for boys. The author has to weave together the threads of the boys, her husband, the employees, the animals, and her own attempts, through it all, to write music.

Some authors before doing their organizing get everything down on paper in narrative form. These authors write up their research as fast as it is done until a full-length manuscript is completed. On the basis of this manuscript the author then selects the threads of interest and fits the material into what seems like the right places. Paragraphs and pages are removed from one place and inserted in another with much discarding, with much further research and writing, and with much rewriting. This method works reasonably well with a book such as a biography, where the organization is simple. With a book which calls for a complicated pattern, the method is not satisfactory. The author wastes too much time in useless labor, and he is always in danger of never ending up with a beautifully organized piece of work. Most successful authors follow outlines. These outlines may be on paper or they may be at least partially in the authors' heads.

As a general rule, the more complicated the pattern the better the book, provided the pattern is not so complicated as to be difficult for the reader to follow. No two books are alike and no instructor can tell an author how to weave the pattern. But an author can study the tapestry of published non-fiction books, he can search for the threads of interest and emotion in his own proposed book, and he can give much thought to their interrelations.

Most of the research problems for a book are the same as those for an article. But the problems of ferreting out the truth often presents greater problems to the book writer. The typical magazine article deals with the near present. The typical book, however, is more likely to deal with the past. What is the truth in bygone days? What is satisfactory evidence of the truth? In a recent manuscript dealing with the old West an author made two statements:

1. That there were fifty million buffalo in 1850 west of the Mississippi. The evidence for this was a dogmatic assertion made by well-known Western authorities.

2. That a steamboat had to wait two days because of an immense number of buffalo who were crossing the Missouri River, impeding the boat's passage. The evidence for this was a quotation from an eyewitness.

The first of these statements may or may not have been true. No census of buffalo was ever taken. No verification is possible. The total number may have been twenty million or one hundred million. The Western authorities thought or guessed that there were fifty million.

The second statement was alleged to have been reported by an eyewitness. This witness may never have said anything of the kind, or he may have told a lie, or he may have exaggerated. Perhaps the eyewitness made the statement quoted, perhaps he was a very reliable witness, but perhaps he had been quoted out of context. Perhaps his complete statement was:

> The steamer was scheduled to sail at seven o'clock in the evening so that there would be time to avoid the shoals and get into deep water before dark. However, innumerable buffalo chose that time to cross the river in front of the boat. This caused the captain to delay departure until the morning. At sunrise a violent easterly storm arose making navigation of the channel dangerous and keeping us tied to our mooring for two days. The appearance of an immense number of buffalo crossing the Missouri at the hour of departure caused our boat to be delayed two days.

The problem of the writer is to seek the truth. What is alleged to be the truth must be tempered by the writer's own judgment of what really happened. Circumstantial evidence, what is probable, may be the truth. A century ago fifty million or a hundred million buffalo may have roamed the old West or held up steamboats for two days, but today, in books, they had better not do so unless the facts are indisputable.

Not only must a lie be avoided, but the reader's credulity must not be unduly strained. A statement must seem true. The Red Queen in *Alice in Wonderland* said she always believed two impossible things each morning before breakfast, but most readers are not like the Red Queen. The seemingly incredible statement must be buttressed by facts or authority so that the reader will believe it. Often the buttressing of a fact is dull and clutters up a manuscript, and it is better to eliminate the statement.

In a scholarly manuscript an author may give his proof in a footnote and thus avoid seeming tedious to the reader. Trevelyan in his *English Social History* makes the following statement: ". . . The Stuart era saw an increase in the coal trade . . ." A footnote gives the figures of coal production in various counties in England before and during the Stuart era. If the figures which prove the statement had been given in the text, they would have been tedious.

A writer should not try to convince a reader of the truth of a statement by saying, "I believe this to be true." Saying such is similar to saying, "I, the author, believe this; you the reader may not." The reader is interested not in the author's belief but in statements that are true per se.

The amount of research necessary for a book is ten to fifty times the amount required for one article. Also, research for a book may wander into bypaths. Samuel Shellabarger, at work on a book about Cortez's conquest of Mexico, stated that he spent three days trying to ascertain one fact. Did Cortez, on his way from Cuba to Mexico, keep his horses on deck or below deck? The fact he was searching for involved one sentence in his book. But his research brought to light new facts about shipboard life in the sixteenth century and enriched his manuscript.

The voluminous research required for a book presents mechanical problems. Where half a dozen folders may be required for research notes on the different subjects pertaining to an article, one hundred folders may be required for a book. Pieces of paper filled with notes may be used, but most writers find cards more practicable. Comprehensive notes save time and avoid errors.

An author, while writing a book about the Mexican War, stated that in 1846 Robert E. Lee was a lieutenant. Actually at this time Lee held the rank of captain. This error caused the author to waste quite a bit of time. When the error was caught, the author made the following explanation: A note pertaining to Stonewall Jackson's rank she had placed by mistake in the Lee research folder. Slipping a card into the wrong folder should have been unimportant. The basic error was the incompleteness of the author's research note. The author's note actually read "Rank Lieutenant in 1846." If the note had read Stonewall Jackson, rank Lieutenant 1846, a misfiling of the note probably would not have occurred. If this more comprehensive note had still gotten into the Lee folder, the error would have been caught when the Lee folder was examined. In either case time would have been saved.

The author's notes in the above were also inadequate in that they failed to give the source of the information. Without the source on each note the author will waste time. He will be unable to check on his own accuracy, insert references in his manuscript, or answer critics without repeating much of the research.

In the writing of a book, the author must keep in mind the amount of space to be used for each phase of the subject. Here the outline is the guide. The proportions of a book should not be determined by the amount of material available or the amount that the author has at his fingertips. It also should not be determined by what interests the author most. In a biography of a U. S. President, there is much less material available on the figure's boyhood than on the period when he was President. This limitation of research material is not the reason why so little space is given in the normal biography to the teen-age years. Less space is given because such years are less important and hence less interesting than when the figure was a prominent and active force.

Suppose an author has uncovered a previously unpublished and unknown diary kept by the figure during several years of his boyhood. If this were Washington's or Lincoln's diary, a book limited to the teen-age years might be a good possibility. Any new extensive material about the most important historical figures arouses public interest. In the case of a complete biography of a minor President such as President Garfield, the author should give no more space to the teen-age years because of finding the diary than he would have given had the diary never been discovered. Due to the diary the author will have a chapter on Garfield's boyhood superior to that of any other biographer. But this chapter should not be any longer. The diary should not alter the proportions of the book.

Revision

Revision for the book is often psychologically difficult. An author preparing an article is bound by the length requirements of a particular magazine. Usually there is a necessity to cut, and the cutting makes him conscious of the revision problem. Also, the rough draft of an article can be read in ten minutes and imperfections may stand out as the author reads. With the book there is a tendency for the author not to do sufficient revision. Finishing the lengthy research, organizing the material, and getting a first draft on paper are such an achievement that the author is apt to rejoice in his success and be tempted to leave well enough alone. The author should realize that much of his work is still before him.

The author should first block out revision as a whole. Perhaps individual chapters are superfluous. Perhaps two chapters could be cut and amalgamated into one. Perhaps a new chapter is needed or perhaps one chapter should be expanded into two. Every author should attempt to suggest to himself work which will bring his book closer to what was originally in his mind's eye.

The next step in revision is that of each individual chapter. Here the article technique may be followed, and every question asked about an article should be asked in the case of each chapter.

In particular, the author should watch for any paragraphs or pages containing unrelated facts. The mind may remember a conclusion, but it remembers few facts. If unrelated facts are presented, there is no conclusion for the reader to remember. The unrelated facts become uninformative and produce dull paragraphs. The solution is elimination of the unrelated, or reorganization so that they are related. Usually both.

Improving the choice of words used, polishing of the English, is the final stage.

No one can say how much revision should be done. Most authors ought to do more than they do. That the quality of published books is below that of published articles is perhaps due to the laziness and weariness of book authors.

Although nine out of ten authors do not do enough revision, a word must be said about the "fiddler," the author who is never satisfied and takes years and years to finish a book, assuming he ever does finish it. The trouble here is that the author has not a clear enough book-idea, does not stick to it, and is making a fetish of writing rather than visualizing his goal, aiming for it, and attaining it.

The Completed Manuscript

After one or more extensive revisions, the writer-in-training prepares an approximately final version of his book. The manuscript is accurately spelled and typed with a minimum of handwritten corrections. The job is done except for one more step. The author should seek criticism.

Many writers-in-training say they want criticism, pretend to themselves they do, but actually do not. They want praise. Criticism can be helpful if the author can avoid having his feelings hurt and make use of it. Praise helps no one. Critics are of two types.

1. The critic for good English, for organization, and for clarity.

Such a critic may be a teacher of English at a high school, a fellow writer, or just someone whom the author thinks is a person of intelligence and good judgment. The critic should not be a close friend or relative, as such usually give nothing but praise.

The author must not expect to get constructive criticism in the sense of being told what to do on the positive side. The critic is not a creator. What the author expects to receive are reactions. He may receive a comment that in certain specific places the manuscript is not clear, or he may receive a comment that certain material is less interesting than other material. The author should reread his manuscript, ponder over the comments. If he finds himself in agreement, clarification and cutting are in order.

Maybe a critic will say of a certain page, "I do not understand this." The author may reply that he has explained that later on in the seventh chapter. The author's answer is unsatisfactory. The reader will not cheerfully wait until the seventh chapter for the explanation. There is an organizational trouble which the author should fix. The second type of critic is:

2. The expert in the area of the manuscript, an authority on the old West for a Western manuscript, a professional bridge player for a manuscript on how to win at bridge, etc.

Books in the information and teaching categories can especially benefit from such expert readings. The author hopes that the critic will catch errors of fact. The critic may also point out places where the authorities disagree and suggest that possibly the author is too dogmatic. The critic may query some of the author's postulates. Here again the author must ponder over the comments. He cannot take everything the critic says as correct or desirable. He must make allowance for pedantry and possible prejudice on the part of the critic. However, every author, as a result of criticism by an expert, can find some changes that will improve his manuscript.

This completes the suggestions on how to write the non-fiction book. There is one other matter which has already been touched upon and should be further explored.

Any discussion of how to write tends to emphasize techniques and is likely to ignore the driving inner force that causes books to be undertaken and completed. The best writing is more than a craft. A bricklayer must lay his bricks properly, and so must a writer build his manuscript, but there is the inspirational factor, and here no teacher of writing can help.

Good books have one thing in common. They are books which the author believes in and feels inspired to write, which are written under a determination and compulsion to overcome all obstacles.

William Shirer had this belief, determination, and compulsion, and wrote *The Rise and Fall of the Third Reich.* He devoted five years to the project under severe financial stress. Shirer was a writer of long experience, he was inspired by a good book-idea, and he produced a work of the first magnitude.

However, the belief, the determination, the compulsion are not enough to insure writing success. In hundreds of cases the compulsion is linked to a poor book-idea, and the result is failure.

In the summer of 1959 a brilliant professional writer from Montana became excited about an airplane episode which occurred to a U. S. Air Force plane. A pilot who should have parachuted to safety took a one percent chance of saving his own life, stayed with the plane, won the odds, and with extraordinary bravery saved the life of his pal. This episode produced a good theme-idea for an article, and *Reader's Digest* and *True* magazine both put staff writers to work on it. The Montana author saw the episode as a book-idea. The agent could not talk him out of it. A young editor of a publishing house offered a contract with money down. Driven by a fantastic compulsion, working night and day, the Montana author wrote up the episode in a brilliant manuscript which he called a book. The manuscript was inevitably too short for a book; the entire episode occurred in an afternoon. There was no way for the manuscript to have a variation of theme, it did not fit into one of the five purpose categories. It was published as a book; it was a failure; it should never have been written.

The agent then gave this author an assignment to work on a good book-idea with money down. He took the job. He was uninspired, unexcited, and under no compulsion to write. The completed manuscript exhibited much honest hard labor, but it was sloppily written. The author had no flair for the subject. The manuscript was published as a book and was a failure. It should never have been written.

If this author had had the compulsion to write a book based upon a good book-idea, he might well have written a best seller. As one best seller begets another, his future would have been bright.

The above example, which repeats itself over and over again, is what makes the world of the written word so frustrating to editors, publishers, literary agents, and teachers of writing. It almost seems as if the linking of an inner compulsion to a good book-idea is in the hands of the gods.

8

BOOKS AUTHORS LIKE TO WRITE

The previous chapter discusses how to write the successful non-fiction book manuscript. This chapter deals with four particular types of manuscripts which are continually written by writers-in-training and which have little chance for success. There are exceptions. No one can say, "Do not write a book in one of these categories." One can only say, "Beware."

The Autobiographical Manuscript

This may be the memoirs of a person's life, the typical autobiography. If such a manuscript is written by a well-known person whose thoughts or accomplishments were noteworthy, it may be fascinating and instructive reading. There is also the partial autobiography. Richard Henry Dana's *Two Years Before the Mast* is an example. Dana was a sailor on a square-rigged ship that sailed from Boston around South America to California and back. His book is a first-person account of two years of his life as a sailor. His fascinating experience resulted in a fascinating book.

Authors of successful autobiographies are apt to be one-book authors. They do not write a second book because they have no further experiences of equal interest. They never become professional writers in the sense of writing and publishing over a continuous period of time.

It is a rare publisher who does not receive each year many autobiographical manuscripts written by people whose names are unknown to the public. One publisher recently received a manuscript entitled *The Autobiography of a Nobody*. A couple of years ago a headwaiter in one of New York's leading hotels wrote of his experiences serving meals to celebrities. When a particular publisher was considering the manuscript, the service given him in the dining room was exceptionally good. Once the publisher declined the manuscript, the service became indifferent.

Many partial memoirs, usually accounts of trite experiences, are submitted to publishers. Their titles may be *My Trip to Europe* or *Camping in the Rockies with Baby and Dog.* Amateurs write books of this autobiographical nature because such books seem so easy to write. The author remembers most of the material, and live and library research seem unnecessary. Any research work is only to jog the memory.

A book project of an autobiographical, or semiautobiographical nature should meet the following conditions:

1. That the author's experiences are so enthralling or unusual or interesting that, if someone else wrote up the identical subject in the third person, a good book would be possible.
2. That there are opportunities for original research, and the author is prepared to do as much research as he would do for any other writing project.

Most writers-in-training have no autobiographical experiences so outstanding as to warrant a book. They are not famous enough so that their life story is of interest to others. Likewise, they do not have any experience so extraordinary or so dangerous or so romantic or so unusual as to warrant a partial autobiography. Moreover, most of these complete or partial autobiographies by unknowns do not lend themselves to research, the basis of most successful books.

As a result, the great mass of these autobiographical manuscripts, just because of content, are not worth the paper they are typed on. The author has selected an unfortunate book-idea. The material is interesting to the author and his family, but to no one else.

There are exceptions. Occasionally a book about a person's trip to Europe is so amusing or so penetrating in its observations of life as to be worthy of publication. Publishers will piously quote, "It all depends upon how well the manuscript is done." In general, when a book describing a trip to Europe is successful, the success is not due to the subject matter. The success is due to the author's use of Europe as a background against which to display his own wit. Some other background would have been as good or better.

Occupation or Hobby Books

This category, akin to autobiography, comprises books about the author's own occupation or hobby. They are very difficult to write successfully. Every person has played a part in some occupation. Perhaps the writer-in-training is a real estate broker or the manager of a store or a digger of septic tanks, or perhaps he is a tournament bridge enthusiast. Conceivably, any of these occupations might offer material for a book.

Writers-in-training often try such a book because they are told, erroneously, to write about what they know, instead of being told, correctly, to know about what they write. Also, such books seem at first blush to require little research work. They seem easy. The pitfall is that most writers-in-training are not experts in anything. It is the old dictum that a little learning is a dangerous thing. A man who has sold real estate or played bridge is not, because of his occupation, an expert. He cannot produce a book on a par with a book written by a true expert.

Genuine experts often write fine books. *The Fannie Farmer Cook Book* is an example. So is Wolfgang Langewiesche's *Stick and Rudder*, the standard book on how to fly an airplane. Expert books may have a wide range. James Thurber was an editor. He did not write an expert book just on his knowledge and experience of editing. He wrote *My Life With Ross.* Ross was the founder and editor-in-chief of *The New Yorker* magazine. Thurber, for many years an editor under Ross, wrote an expert's book about Ross, the editor.

The true expert has an advantage in that he has acquired and absorbed much of the material before he ever imagined writing a book. He has a feel for his material and a judgment derived from practical experience. Over the years he has developed and tested a point of view.

If the expert will do research as he writes, testing his theories and filling in the gaps in his knowledge (no expert knows everything about his subject), he will produce a better book. If an expert just relies on his own knowledge and experience, he may write a good book, never the best possible. In *My Life With Ross,* Thurber tells of the large amount of research work he undertook.

"Nut" Books

These are books which seem to the reader unimportant or absurd. Many people, otherwise of good judgment, write books of this ilk. The subject matter of "nut" books may be almost anything, but at times they seem to follow a fashion. At one time books with themes about the lost continent of Atlantis were being written by the dozens.

Recently an author wrote a manuscript to demonstrate that the man who shot Abraham Lincoln did not have the name of Booth, and was not the brother of the actor, Edwin Booth. This manuscript is in the "nut" category. Suppose the author's facts are irrefutable and his supposition is true? Most readers will still refuse to be persuaded. The historical statement that a man named Booth killed Lincoln has become ingrained in their thoughts or, if you will, in their prejudices. Also, to most readers the matter does not seem of any importance. Who cares what the name of the assassin was? Why read a book about the subject?

A book to the effect that Francis Bacon was the author of Shakespeare's plays is not in this category. There has been so much previously published on the question as to who wrote the plays attributed to Shakespeare that readers will not reject the author's thesis as absurd. Also, the discussion is, at least to the scholar, important.

There is no way of devising a yardstick to determine whether a book-idea is in the "nut" area. Just because an author wants to persuade others to his way of thinking, and just because he believes that his crusade, so important to him, is important to others, his opinion as to the appeal of such a book is apt to be faulty. The instructor can only plead for good judgment.

Publicity and Propaganda Books

In this category is the large area of writing which is called "publicity" if one wants to praise it, and "propaganda" if one wants to disparage it. A history of a business corporation, published for the sake of good public relations, is an example of the publicity book. A book prepared by the Birch Society or by the Communists is an example of the propaganda book. These publicity and propaganda books are a bastard form of non-fiction. Their contents are not confined to the truth.

We have spoken in an earlier chapter of how the search for truth should dominate all non-fiction writing. The truth is more than just avoiding sentences that lie. The truth implies an attempt at impartiality, an attempt not only to write true sentences and paragraphs but to give an overall portrayal of what is true. A book can lie because of omissions or unfair emphasis. Granted that the truth is a matter of degree, is seen darkly as through a glass, and means different things to different people. Still, without an honest search for truth, the non-fiction writer has nothing. This does not mean that any one manuscript is an attempt to cover all the truth about a subject. Every book is an attempt to portray only a segment of the truth. If an author is writing a book about the achievements of the American woman, he may well ignore a discussion of notorious prostitutes. A discussion of prostitutes does not fit into his book-idea; hence, they are not part of his area of truth. If an author is writing a book on the favorable and unfavorable influence of women upon men, a discussion of prostitutes must be included. In each case the author is actuated by an attempt to portray the truth within the confines of his book-idea.

An author writing publicity, such as the history of a business corporation, avoids any overt lies and seems to keep within the bounds of truth, but his primary motive is to produce a book which will be good publicity for the business. The publicity motive is never completely compatible with the truth motive.

There are books in the publicity field which make a contribution to the affairs of this world. A book in behalf of the Salvation Army or a book sponsored by the National Safety Council in behalf of national safety would be examples. The extent to which such books deviate from the search for the truth may be slight, but almost always there is a deviation.

An author writing a propaganda book is usually an avid believer in his crusade. Consciously or unconsciously he feels that the end justifies the means. Persuading people to his own beliefs is so important to him that individual lies or overall lying becomes unimportant to him. The propaganda motive becomes supreme. The search for truth becomes quiescent.

A few propaganda books are greeted with wild acclaim by adherents of that which is advocated. Certainly *Das Kapital* by Karl Marx or *Mein Kampf* by Adolf Hitler have changed history.

Professional writers rarely write propaganda books. Only a fanatic can write a good one, and most writers are not fanatics. Occasionally a corporation will offer a professional writer a large sum to write their history. Occasionally an individual will do the same to get his biography written. Such books may get published; in nine cases out of ten they are failures. The publishers make money because the corporation or person who paid the author to write the book also pays the publisher by purchasing many copies to give away. Professional writers with the highest sense of writing integrity refuse to be wooed by money and will not write these books. They write books based on their own book-ideas and are actuated solely by a search for the truth.

9

MARKETING THE BOOK

The author of a non-fiction book should have in mind publication in hard covers at a retail price of $3.50 or up. If the book has a successful hard-cover sale, it may be reprinted in a paperback edition. First publication in paperback is occurring with certain types of books, and this practice is likely to become more common in the future. As of today the author in most cases should look for the traditional hard-cover publication.

Usually a professional writer tries to interest a publisher in his book project long before the manuscript is completed. Once he has selected his book-idea and has done preliminary research, he prepares an outline. This may be in a form similar to an article outline or may be in the form of chapter headings, that is, a short description of what is to be in each chapter. The author then encloses the outline with a letter addressed to a publisher asking the publisher if he is interested. In the letter of inquiry the author may mention the live and library research he plans to undertake. He may mention his writing past and why he feels competent to do the book. He may mention other books in the field and suggest how his book will differ from what has been previously published.

The writer-in-training who has no publishing connections should show his outline to any one of the large, well-known publishers such as Harper & Row, Doubleday & Co., and Macmillan, who publish a large number of non-fiction titles of a general nature. If the proposed book is specialized, for example a manuscript on flower arranging, a publisher who has published books in that field may be a more likely possibility. However, the large houses publish a great variety of subjects.

An author can expect an answer to his letter of inquiry within two weeks. The publisher may reply that he is uninterested, in which case the author will try someone else. The publisher may offer the author a contract. This is unlikely at this stage unless the author has one or more previously published books which have enjoyed at least modest success. The publisher may ask to see one or several sample chapters and offer to contract if such chapters seem to him satisfactory. This is what writers-in-training hope for.

In general, it is no more difficult to obtain a book contract on the basis of sample chapters and an outline than it is with a completed manuscript. The situation is different with a novel. Fiction can open well and in subsequent chapters fall to pieces. With a non-fiction book, if the book-idea is interesting, if the outline and sample chapters are well organized and well written, the author should be able to maintain the quality in subsequent chapters. The publisher's risk of getting a poor manuscript is not great.

Sample chapters should be the opening chapters of the book in consecutive order, with the balance in outline form. The publisher cannot form an intelligent opinion on the basis of excerpts from the middle of the book. The sample chapters should be in final polished form, as good as the author can make them. As in the case of an article, no first draft should ever be offered. The publisher will render an opinion on the basis of the words on the submitted typed pages. He will not assume that at some later date the sample chapters will be improved. Likewise, much care and thought should be put into the outline. The outline is to persuade the publisher that the author has enough material for a book and knows how to organize a book. The fact that the outline will be subject to minor changes as the book progresses does not warrant submitting a sloppy, off-the-top-of-the-head outline.

Usually an author finds it necessary to complete the major portion of his research in order to write the opening chapters, and in order to prepare a satisfactory outline. The author must research what will be in the latter part of a book because that affects the opening chapters. An author must research all the various threads of interest in order to show in outline their interrelations.

If a manuscript cannot be sold to a legitimate publisher on a royalty basis, it should be put in an attic and forgotten. The only exception is in the case of a learned, or scientific, or exceedingly scholarly manuscript where a publisher, often a university press, may require some outside financing in order to undertake publication.

There are pseudo publishers who call themselves "cooperative" publishers and whom the publishing trade calls "vanity" publishers. Authors should have nothing to do with these publishing sharks, who persuade authors to pay them $2000 and up (depending upon the length of the manuscript) to finance the publication of the author's book. The publishing shark then arranges for the manufacture of the book, and offers to pay the author a fantastically high royalty, often 40 percent of the retail price on each copy sold. The catch is that few if any books sponsored by a vanity publisher earn any appreciable royalty. They are not sold to the public. The books that these sharks publish are in most cases poor to illiterate, and no one wants to buy them. If, by some fluke, the author of a good manuscript pays one of these sharks, the book is not sold to the public, because these publishers have little intent and no organization to sell books. The author who goes to a vanity publisher gets nicely bound copies of his book which have cost him a pretty penny. These he can give away to his friends. That is all. He has wasted his money and has in no respect forwarded his career. The author could have achieved the same result, with just as remote a possibility of success and with a considerable saving of money, if he had arranged directly with a printer for the manufacture of his book.

An author can expect a reply to a submission of sample chapters and outline within a month. Repeated rejections mean that the book-idea is poor or that the sample chapters are badly organized and written or that the author has an ineffective outline. The fundamental reason for rejections often is that the author has not yet learned his trade as a writer.

When an author is proffered a contract by a publisher he will receive a document of monstrous verbosity. The Simon & Schuster contract, the most verbose of all, contains 12,000 words; the more typical Harper & Row contract, over 3000 words. These printed-form contracts ask the author to turn over to the publisher most or all rights to the manuscript. The following are the major rights:

> The right to turn the manuscript into a book and sell the book in bookstores.
>
> The right to arrange with a book club for the sale of the book by mail.
>
> The right to arrange (usually with a different publisher) for a reprint paperback edition of the book.
>
> The right to arrange for an edition with a British publisher, and for editions in translation with foreign publishers.
>
> The right to arrange for a motion picture, television performance, or dramatic show based upon the book.
>
> The right to sell the book, or part of it, to magazines or newspapers before or after book publication.

In exchange for these rights the publisher agrees to have the manuscript printed and manufactured as a book; he agrees to put the book on sale in the United States and Canada and distributed through bookstores; and he agrees to pay the author a royalty on every copy sold to the public. The publisher further agrees to pay a sum of money as an advance against this hoped-for royalty. With respect to the other rights the publisher agrees to pay the author a percentage of the money the publisher collects.

Obtaining a contract with a legitimate publisher before the author's manuscript is completed is encouraging. The contract is concrete evidence that the author has a good book-idea. It encourages the author to continue the arduous, time-consuming process of producing a book. It also gives the author some money down (usually a relatively small sum). A further advantage is that the publisher may have editorial suggestions which will improve the book. Such suggestions could be made after the manuscript has been completed, but time and labor may be saved if the suggestions are received at an earlier stage.

Signing a contract before completion of the manuscript does not ensure publication. The usual book contract calls for the delivery of a manuscript "satisfactory to the publisher in form and content." The publisher has to read and approve the final manuscript before he is obligated to publish. Even if the contract unconditionally obligates the publisher to publish, there is no practical way of compelling him to. Moreover, the author would have little to gain in obtaining publication from a publisher who does not believe in the author's book. Such a publisher is not likely to sell the book to the public.

What usually happens when the publisher does not like the completed work is that the author or his agent tries to find a new publisher. If this is successful, the contract with the first publisher is canceled, and a contract is entered into with the new publisher. The author pays back the first publisher out of money collected from the new publisher. If the author is unsuccessful in finding a new publisher, the manuscript is never published, the author retaining the money received from the first publisher.

When a publisher accepts a manuscript, he may have editorial suggestions which he hopes, if followed, will improve the manuscript. He may also suggest a different title from what the author has suggested. The manuscript incorporating any further changes the author has made is then copyedited. This means that spelling, punctuation, and grammar are corrected and made to conform to the publisher's house rules. Sometimes the author's English is improved. Questionable statements of fact are checked and, if need be, corrected. The author receives a set of galleys to correct. With the best will in the world there are always some printing errors and some queries to the author as to what he meant to write.

Along with this printing process the publisher prepares a jacket, prepares material for his salesmen and for trade publications, lists the book in his catalog, and a month or so before the publication date sends copies gratis to book reviewers throughout the country. The publisher's publicity director may send out news releases about the author or the book. The advertising manager may, in collaboration with an advertising agency, prepare a couple of small advertisements; or, if the book looks like a best seller, a large advertising campaign may be planned.

The publisher's salesmen travel from bookstore to bookstore offering the book along with others on the publisher's list. Finally, six to nine months after delivery of the manuscript, publication day arrives. Reviews in newspapers and magazines begin to trickle in. Either the public begins to buy and the bookstores order further copies or the public does not buy and the unsold books are returned to the publisher.

Public acceptance or rejection is the test of success or failure. What agents, publishers, or friends of the author have said about the book becomes of no importance. The author has written and marketed a book. The public is the court of last resort.

We have discussed what happens to the author with a book contract from the time of completion of his manuscript to book publication. Many book authors retain a literary agent. There are some one hundred so-called literary agents listed in the New York telephone book, and maybe another twenty-five so-called literary agents with residences outside New York City. These so-called literary agents may be divided into two groups: on the one hand, the legitimate author's representative; on the other, the pseudo literary agent. Pseudo agents are the fee chargers, the advertisers, the literary sharks in the same bed with the vanity publishers. They make their money from checks paid to them by authors, not from commissions on sales made for authors. Most pseudo agents make few if any sales, despite their testimonial advertising.

There are thirty-six legitimate agents who are members of the Society of Author's Representatives. All of the members of the Society are believed to be honest and competent. There are only two or three agents of good reputation who have not joined the Society.

Legitimate agents work on a 10 percent commission basis. They negotiate the contract, collect the money from the buyer, and pay 90 percent to the author. They handle all the business paper work for the author. They make many contracts or sales where the author would have done just as well on his own, and the author is the poorer by 10 percent. They may make a sale or so handle a contract that the author is substantially richer despite the commission. A good agent is more than a negotiator. He is a man experienced in the editorial and business side of writing whose advice may be of value. In what ways does an author at times seek advice?

In the case of any book there is a continual series of decisions to be made. The author can leave these to the publisher. Many authors, at least after their first book, consult a literary agent. They want to be in on these decisions themselves. What are the decisions?

The first is the book-idea. Is it a good one? Some authors instinctively select good ones. Many do not. An author can consult his publisher, but he is in the position of wanting to sell his publisher, and selling and consulting may be contradictory. Many an author consults his agent as to the possibilities of a book-idea.

Another decision is how much of the manuscript must be written in order to obtain a desirable contract and a determination of the approximate final length of the book when completed. With the article the editor's interest is obtained through an outline, and the final length is determined by the requirements of the magazine. Books vary. Some can be sold on the basis of an outline alone, some require a couple of sample chapters, some require much more of the book on paper. The ultimate length of the complete book manuscript is flexible and in great measure should be determined by the nature and amount of the material. But the book must be long enough to satisfy the public, and yet not so long as to grow dull to the reader or to necessitate too high a retail price.

There are some 70 trade book publishers listed in the New York telephone book, and there are many others scattered around the country, with some important ones in Boston, Philadelphia, and Chicago. What publisher should the author choose? In the case of a large number of books the publisher is already selected. Perhaps a publisher has an option on the manuscript in question, or perhaps the author desires a particular publishing house because he has a personal relationship to a particular editor. However, the author often has a choice at the start, and usually during his career he shifts his publisher several times.

The author may select his publisher through the recommendation of some friend, or he may select the publisher through whim or hunch. Harry Overstreet, the author of *The Mature Mind*, a book that had an enormous sale, chose Norton as his publisher because the president of Norton beat him at badminton on shipboard. One author who became very successful, Bess Streater Aldrich, obtained an alphabetical list of publishers from her library, and offered her first book to Appleton because that publisher headed the list.

Some authors consult an agent as to the selection of a publisher; some leave the selection entirely to the agent.

There is no such thing as the best publisher in the United States, any more than there is such a thing as the best garage in the United States. The leading agents divide publishers into three classes:

1. First-class publishers.
2. Adequate publishers.
3. Poor publishers that the agent does not place a book with if he can avoid it.

First-class publishers have plenty of money to promote a book which the public begins to buy. They have an efficient organization, a strong sales force, and know-how concerning the promotion and launching of a book. They tend to offer the author a favorable contract.

Publishers in the second class fail in one or more of these requirements.

Publishers in the third class may be two or three people who occasionally publish a book as a hobby (anyone can be a publisher if he has some money to lose). Publishers in this class may be of some size, but they obtain books at terms disadvantageous to the author and may display incredible ineptitude and inefficiency in the promotion and sale of a book.

It is a matter of judgment and degree as to what class a publisher is placed in. Doubtless a publisher in Class 1 on some leading agents' lists would be in Class 2 on others, but there is general agreement. A publisher in Class 3 on one leading agent's list would never be in Class 1 on another leading agent's list.

The decision as to the publisher may involve the choice of an editor. Some authors want a young, energetic editor, some an older one whom they feel will be wiser. Some do not like a woman editor. Theoretically, race or religion should not enter in, but people are people, and some authors, Jewish and Gentile, have a preference for a Jewish or Gentile editor. The first impulse of many writers-in-training is to see if they can work with the publisher's editor-in-chief, and most editors-in-chief do personally take care of some authors who are relatively unknown. However, the editor-in-chief of a large house has so many administrative duties, so many conferences that he must attend, so much traveling to do, that his authors, unless their sales are very large, may find their books neglected. An assiduous under-editor may follow a book more closely from manuscript to publication and be of more value to the book than the editor-in-chief. In all of these matters the author may make his own decision, or may consult the agent, or may leave it up to the agent to use his own judgment.

The terms in a proffered book contract require decisions on the part of the author.

The important terms in a book contract are:

1. The size of the advance.
2. The royalty rate and the circumstances under which it may be reduced.
3. The rights the author is selling to the publisher, and what percent of the revenue from the sale of such rights will accrue to the author.
4. To what extent the author is bound by option to the publisher if he writes further books.

It is with regard to these four categories that bargaining is involved and that decisions must be made. All the other multitudinous clauses in the publisher's form contract have been drawn by the publisher's lawyer, and are weighted in the publisher's favor, but the amounts of money involved are usually small.

Decisions with Regards to the Size of the Advance

With a first book or a book by an author whose previous books have had modest sales, how much money a publisher will advance is usually a matter of persuasion. Most publishers, if pressed, will increase their first offer slightly. If an author is hard up and willing to admit it, he can often get more money than otherwise. If the research work involved heavy expenses for the author, such may be a basis for increasing the advance. If the book-idea intrigues the editor and the author seems especially competent to write on the subject, sometimes quite a few thousand dollars can be obtained even though the author has no previous book record. With a best-selling author, agents may go from publisher to publisher to see who will advance the most. As this volume goes to press, Mary Martin has been offered an advance of $60,000, and the ultimate figure will probably be higher. More than $100,000 in advance against royalty has been paid for a non-fiction book.

There are a handful of publishers whose form contract contains a clause calling for repayment of the advance if the publisher does not like the completed manuscript. An author has to decide whether to try to get such a clause deleted from the contract. In 1957 a successful women's magazine writer signed a contract with the well-known publishing house of Henry Holt & Co. to write a non-fiction book. Her contract called for an advance against royalty of $1000 payable upon the signing of the instrument, and a second $1000 payable upon receipt of a completed manuscript satisfactory to the publisher in form and content. Everything was signed and the first $1000 duly paid. The author did not notice a sentence in small type (practically everything in a book contract is printed in small type) to the effect that if the publisher did not like the completed manuscript the author must immediately pay back the first $1000 and the contract would be rescinded. Research for this non-fiction book was completed and, after months of labor, the book was finished. The publisher did not like the manuscript and demanded his money back. The author could not sell the manuscript elsewhere and had no recourse but to refund it.

Had the publisher been completely candid, had he written her a letter saying that he would loan her $1000 without interest, that if he liked the book she could keep the money, otherwise she must return it, perhaps the contract would never have been signed. Of course, the author should have read the contract carefully before signing. After all, writers are supposed to be highly literate people. Henry Holt & Co. (now Holt, Rinehart & Winston) have revised their form contract and no longer have this clause for the return of the advance if they do not like the completed manuscript. But there are other publishers who have such a clause.

Decisions To Be Made Concerning Royalty Rate

The contract proffered by the publisher may call for a royalty on a sliding scale: 10 percent of the retail price on the first 5000 copies sold, 12½ percent on the next 5000 copies sold, and 15 percent thereafter. This is a favorable royalty. The new writer cannot hope for any better, and he may have to take a lesser royalty, perhaps 10 percent of the retail price on the first 10,000 copies, and 12½ percent thereafter. The above refers to the official royalty rate. The danger is that there may be a clause somewhere else in the contract which limits the official rate, a clause which in the case of a particular book may have the effect of reducing the author's total revenue severely.

A publisher sells his books to bookstores and to wholesalers at a discount. Suppose the publisher gives the bookstores a 40 percent discount. This means that the bookstore buys from the publisher for $2.40 a book retailing at $4.00. The bookstore makes a $1.60 profit when it sells the book to a customer. The publisher has $2.40 to pay his expenses and the author's royalty. However, discounts vary. There may be a clause in the author's contract which provides that if the publisher sells the book at a discount of 50 percent or more, the author is entitled not to 10 percent of the retail price but to only 10 percent of what the publisher receives. Suppose the publisher sells the $4.00 book to the bookstores for $2.00. The official clause in the contract calls for a royalty of 10 percent of the retail price or $.40 a copy. Due to the limiting clause the author actually receives 10 percent of what the publisher collects or only $.20 a copy. Of course the publisher who has such a limiting clause in his contract may not sell at a discount of 50 percent or more or he may sell only a very few copies at the 50 percent or more discount. However the clause may be invoked in the case of certain books so that the author's royalty revenue may be reduced by an amount ranging anywhere from one fifth to one half of what he would have received had the limiting clause not been in the contract. The author Howard Fast estimated that the royalty on one of his books was reduced more than a fourth by such a clause. Printed in the Appendix is a clause of this nature. Also included in the Appendix is a clause from the form contract of William Morrow and Company, which clause the author of this volume recommends. Every author has to decide to what extent he will press for a favorable clause covering this matter.

Decisions To Be Made with Regard to Rights to the Manuscript

A publisher's form contract usually gives him most, if not all, rights to the author's manuscript. However, nearly every publisher in the first and second classes will relinquish some of the rights and discuss the author's interest in some of the remaining rights. There are two rights the publisher inevitably retains. One is the right to sell the author's manuscript to a book club for distribution by mail. The other is the right to sell the manuscript to a paperback publisher (sometimes to a subsidiary of his own) for distribution at a cheap price on newsstands. It is the practice for the publisher and the author to split the revenue from these rights fifty-fifty. No publisher will consider or discuss paying the author a larger percentage.

In the case of four out of five published books no book club is interested and the rights cannot be sold. When there is a book club selection, the amount of the revenue depends upon how large the club is and upon the club's success in selling by mail the book in question.

Book club revenue runs from a minimum of $1000 to a maximum, in one or two cases a year, of over $100,000. Paperback revenue may be non-existent or may run from a $1000 to the phenomenal $400,000 paid for *The Rise and Fall of the Third Reich*. Through complicated methods, beyond the scope of this volume, a few writers with big names, whose books are of enormous value, are somewhat breaking down the fifty-fifty split on paperback revenue. All writers-in-training and nine out of ten successful professional writers have to split this revenue fifty-fifty.

Motion Picture, Television, and Dramatic Rights

Most, but not all, first-class publishers will readily relinquish any interest in these rights if requested. Some publishers in the third class ask for 50 percent. Many in the second and a few in the first class ask for from 10 percent to 25 percent. The publisher usually uses an agent to sell the rights and takes his share after deducting the agent's commission. Most publishers will not refuse to publish a book if they are deprived of these rights. However, the matter is not of great importance. Motion picture rights on only a handful of non-fiction books are sold each year. Television has shown increased interest in non-fiction, but there is little likelihood that this medium will use a substantial percent of published titles in the foreseeable future. Non-fiction books are seldom suitable for a Broadway dramatization.

British Empire and Translation Rights

If the publisher retains these he usually sells them through an agent, and after deducting the agent's commission, retains from 25 percent to 50 percent for himself, paying the balance to the author. For example, in the case of *Moulin Rouge* by Pierre La Mure, the publishers, Random House, placed the foreign rights in the hands of the well-known agent Curtis Brown. Curtis Brown put the translation rights in the hands of sub-agents. The sub-agents took a 10 percent commission, Curtis Brown took 10 percent of the remaining 90 percent, so that 81 percent was left. Random House retained 25 percent of the 81 percent, so that the author received about 60 percent of a total of over $50,000 of translation money.

If the author uses an agent, most publishers in the first and second classes will relinquish any interest in translation rights. However, there is no practical way for an author to market these rights except through an agent or through his publisher.

Perhaps half of the books published in the United States are never sold abroad. The other half are sold to one or more countries, bringing a total revenue of from $250 to $5000, best sellers excepted. These may produce a phenomenal translation revenue.

First and Second Serial Rights

First serial rights are the right to publish the manuscript in whole or in part in a magazine or newspaper before book publication. With the exception of publishers in the third class, few ask for an interest in these rights. If the publisher does want them, or if the author wants the publisher to handle them, the publisher will usually do so on a 10 percent commission basis.

First serial rights of a book of general interest may be sold to such magazines as *Reader's Digest, Look,* or one of the women's magazines. A book of purely masculine interest may be sold to such magazines as *True* or *Argosy*. Occasionally a non-fiction book is serialized in its entirety. Sometimes it will be condensed and published in one issue of a magazine. Sometimes one chapter will be lifted from the manuscript and published as an article. This may require extra work on the part of the author to cut and rework the chapter to meet the magazine's requirements. Prices may run from $2000 to $10,000 an installment, or even higher, depending upon the magazine, the material, and how well the author is known. First serial rights to the memoirs of a President might bring a half million dollars or more.

First serial rights to a specialized book may be possible for a specialized magazine. A book on fishing might well have a chapter that *Field and Stream* or *Outdoor Life* would be interested in. Here the revenue to the author would be small, perhaps $200 or $300. However, the magazine will refer to the chapter as an excerpt from a forthcoming book, and such publicity may help the publisher to get the book known to the public and thereby increase its sale. The number of specialized markets is so large and covers such a wide variety of interests that no author should assume that no magazine possibilities exist. The author should hunt for publications that might be interested in one of his chapters.

Decisions To Be Made with Regard to Options on Future Books

Here is another area where authors often fare badly. The form contract proffered to an author for his first book may give the publisher an option to publish the author's next two books on the same terms as the first. This option clause does not require the publisher to accept and publish the author's next two books. It does require the author to offer the publisher his next two books when he finishes them. No matter how good commercially the succeeding books are, and no matter how well-known the author has become, if the publisher insists, the author must sell the publisher these books on the same terms as the first book. The terms for the first book may have been unfavorable, but the unpublished author felt he had to accept. Or the terms for the first book may have been favorable, considering the manuscript, but in the case of the two following books the terms may be unfavorable and substantially less than what some other publisher would offer. Publishers in the first class and many in the second class will offer an option clause for the next one or two books at terms to be arranged, that is to say, the author does not have to accept the same terms as his previous book, but can negotiate for improvement. Every author has to decide how long and on what terms he is willing to be tied to his publisher.

When the author has finished his manuscript to his own satisfaction, and his publisher has accepted it, there are usually editorial matters for decision.

Most publishers offer editorial suggestions, some major, some trivial. The author wants his manuscript to be as good as possible. He must decide to what extent the publisher is right. He must also decide whether the criticism is important enough to justify the labor of rewriting. He must also consider whether he can do satisfactorily what the publisher suggests. It is easy for the author to remind himself that he is the creator. Why should an editor, who is not a writer, tell him what to do? Certainly many books whose authors had refused to follow an editor's advice have become best sellers. Likewise, many an author who has revised according to an editor's directions, dotted every *i* and crossed every *t* as requested, has found himself the author of an unsuccessful book. However, the above statements are deceiving. The author is the trained creator of manuscripts; the editor is the trained critic of manuscripts. In four out of five cases the best manuscript results from the combined contributions of editor and author, and in four out of five cases the best manuscripts have the best sales.

In considering criticism the author should try to visualize what the editor feels is the trouble, and then try to find ways of improvement. The editor may make constructive suggestions which would improve the manuscript. The author's own constructive ideas on the same points are apt to be superior to what the publisher can suggest. If the author, after much consideration, cannot see the trouble, no change should be made. The editor may be wrong. If the editor is right but the author cannot visualize the trouble, revision is unlikely to be successful. The agent is often consulted as a second editor. Usually he agrees with the editor. Sometimes he agrees but doubts if the trouble is sufficiently important. Occasionally he disagrees. Some editors, usually the very young ones, get editorialitis and criticize any and all manuscripts regardless of their merit, and the agent's advice may be of a restraining nature.

Titles are a continual matter of discussion and sometimes of dispute between author and publisher. With an article, the editors pick and use a title without consulting or even informing the author. With a book, the author is supposed to have the final say. What is a good title? The name of most products is unimportant. If Henry Ford's name had been Henry Jones, people would merrily buy a Jones car. A magazine can have a meaningful title like *The New Yorker*. It can also have a meaningless title like *McCall's*. The millions of copies printed each month give currency and meaning to the name *McCall's*. But it is the overwhelming opinion of the publishers and sellers of books that titles are important.

A book, unlike a magazine, is individual. A name for an

individual, if the name is to be publicized, can be important. If Adolf Hitler had kept his real name, Adolf Schicklgruber, would not history have been changed? Did Adlai Stevenson's mother do him a favor by naming him Adlai? In 1962 including fiction and every type of non-fiction, 16,448 different titles were issued. This is the equivalent of almost 320 titles each week. No publisher has the money to develop and turn into a household word any one title. Nevertheless each book has to be promoted so that the public will buy at least some copies. In connection with this promotion, the title is either a hindrance or a help. A good title makes it easier to write effective jacket copy and to produce effective publicity and advertising. What is a good title? It is not one that is considered all alone, as if in a vacuum. A good title is one that fits into or sums up or will look well or sound well on a jacket, in reviews, and in promotion and advertising copy.

A title should be short so that it can be easily remembered. No one would use ten words for the name of a car or of a magazine. A title should be reasonably easy to say, not a tongue-twister. Spain has two provinces, Aragon and Castile. Samuel Shellabarger wanted to call his famous novel *Captain From Aragon,* as his hero came from that province. His publisher and agent persuaded him to entitle the book *Captain From Castile.* The alliteration makes the title *Captain From Castile* easier to say and remember.

A title should not be composed of trite-sounding words. They are too easy for the reader to forget. *A Beautiful Day* would not be a good title: *The Female Parent* might be. The agent for Mary O'Hara suggested *A Summer at the Ranch* as a title for her book. The publisher suggested *Wyoming Summer* as shorter and less trite-sounding, and this publisher's suggestion was an improvement.

A title should have a relation to the tone of the book. A humorous book should not have a deadly serious title, or vice versa. A how-to-do-it book is helped by a title which describes its purpose and contents. The volume that the reader is now reading is entitled *The Writing and Selling of Non-Fiction,* a descriptive title. Suppose the title page read *Thoughts* by Paul R. Reynolds? With such a title the publisher would have nothing to help him sell the book, and publishers need every bit of help they can get to sell books. The agent, as a friend at court and presumably of good judgment in the affairs of the written word, is often consulted and makes suggestions as to the title.

All of the above decisions can be left to the discretion of the publisher, or they can be made by author and publisher in consultation, or a middle man, an agent, can be retained. Whether to employ an agent or not is a matter each author must decide. Some authors want someone to help them make the decisions. Many authors do not want this help or feel they can get it direct from their publisher.

Many authors want an agent to negotiate the terms of their contract with the publisher. No agent can get an author better terms than an astute author can obtain for himself. The agent has no magic, and no publisher will pay the agent better terms than he will pay the author direct. However, a large number of authors feel incapable of bargaining with their publisher. They can bargain over the sale of their own house or their own car, but not over their literary brainchild. Also, many authors are too close to their own work to evaluate it, and are too ignorant to know what is important in their contract and what is unimportant.

The motion picture rights to a book are almost universally handled by an agent. An author would not know to whom to offer his book or what to charge. Some motion picture and television buyers will only read material submitted through an agent.

As a result of all this, the use of the agent has become common with the popular type of general non-fiction. Theoretically there should be no need for a middle man, a 10 percent parasite. Theoretically no authors should need them and few should use them. But with a continually changing publishing world, and a world that each year seems to get more complicated, the agent is a factor in the careers of many professional writers.

10

WHAT PUBLISHING A BOOK IS LIKE

The writing and publishing of books should be the goal of every article writer. There are two reasons for this. In the first place the book writer is under far less stress. The book author need find only one or perhaps two good book-ideas a year, while the article writer must find anywhere from ten to twenty good theme-ideas a year. Research for a 100,000-word book is concentrated. The research for 50,000 words of articles is distributed over ten or twenty usually unrelated subjects. As the article writer gets older, the strain of the article rat race becomes more severe.

The second reason for getting into the book field is the possibilities it offers for money and fame. The financial rewards for the most successful article writer are limited, and there is little fame or reputation in his occupation. There is almost no limitation to the possibilities of fame and money in the book field.

Desirable as it is to write a book, an article writer should not kid himself and pretend that something is a book when it is not. A collection of non-fiction articles which previously appeared in magazines is not a book. If the collection is published as a book, it still remains articles bound together in book form. Likewise, expanding an article into book length has its dangers. It may remain only an expanded article.

Geoffrey Hellman, the distinguished *New Yorker* writer, will have a collection of his articles published in book form in 1963. They will not be a book. He wrote a profile for *The New Yorker* on the Guggenheims. Can he write a book about the Guggenheims? Of course he can and a dozen publishers would jump to give him a contract. The danger in the project is that it may seem easy, just an expanding of his *New Yorker* piece. No blowing up of that piece will do. For a good book the author would have to start from scratch, do the amount of research, organization, and writing that would be necessary had he never written the *New Yorker* profile.

The transition from article writing to book writing should be gradual, and it is never easy. Many a full-time article writer finds it difficult to earn the $10,000 or $12,000 necessary to support his family in the way they want to live. He dares not slack off on his article writing to gamble the time necessary to complete a book. Supporting one's family must come first, but every writer, part time or full time, can devote one afternoon or one evening or one day a week to working on a book. If the writer makes himself do this, in all probability five years later he will be glad he did so.

The segment of the book industry that sells books in hard covers to the public through bookstores has changed little in the last one hundred years. The business is customrid and is managed on old-fashioned and unscientific lines. Nearly every phase of American business has gone through a period of extraordinary change and development. The book industry, small, inefficient, with individual businesses often run by rich amateurs as a hobby, has ambled along, letting the rest of the world pass them by. This is changing. Since the Second World War selling books in mass quantities in paperback, and selling hard-cover books in mass quantities by mail, have developed into big business. Scientific methods are being introduced. This bookselling explosion may ultimately kill, certainly will change, the distribution of books via the bookstores. As of now the book business of publisher selling to the public via the bookstore remains as heretofore, and is the road to fame and money for the author.

A total of 16,448 new books in all categories were published in 1962. Subtracting from this figure the number of books in the classifications of fiction, juveniles, law, medicine, music, poetry and drama, technical books, textbooks, and translations, leaves a total of 7822 non-fiction books, most of which could have been written by the average professional writer or writer-in-training. Ninety-five percent of these books were first published in hard covers and sold primarily through bookstores.

No figures are available as to the amount of money earned by the authors of these books. The amount a publisher pays an individual author is confidential. Moreover, any one book may earn royalty for many years, or it may go out of print and later be republished, paying further royalty long after the first publication. It may earn money from sources other than the American publisher, and this may occur years after the first publication.

The author of this volume has estimated the earnings of the non-fiction writer on the basis of his own experience with the business affairs of authors and the estimates made by publishers. He believes that his figures are underestimates. However, the reader must take these figures as a guess, although possibly an educated guess.

Authors of the 7822 non-fiction books published in 1962 will average more than $3500 a book, so that the total earnings of all these 7822 books will exceed $27,000,000. This amount will be distributed somewhat as follows:

50	authors earned or will earn more than	$50,000 from one book
250	authors earned or will earn more than	20,000 from one book
2000	authors earned or will earn more than	4,000 from one book
5500	authors earned or will earn less than	4,000 from one book

Obviously, five out of seven of these writers will be poorly paid for the time and labor expended. This is characteristic of the writing trade in all mediums.

Lack of success with a book is often a severe emotional blow to the author. Publication day is the start of what the author hopes will be mass distribution of his product. The day arrives for the author like any other day. His publisher may telegraph congratulations, which gives the author something to paste in his scrapbook. The author's friends are ignorant of his book unless his wife has talked about it, and none of them have read it or will read it. If the author lives in a small town and his publisher or his wife has taken the trouble, there will be a glowing article in the local paper, and the local library or drug store will have some copies, most of which will not be purchased or read. As the days go by, reviews trickle in from various parts of the country. In every case the reviews are short, sometimes just a mention of the book. Usually they are favorable. The publisher perhaps takes one small advertisement in the New York *Times* Book Review section. The author waits and hopes; nothing more happens. The author blames his publisher for not advertising his book. ("How can my book sell if no one knows about it?") The author blames his publisher because, on a trip to Chicago, he found three bookstores who did not have a single copy of his book. Perhaps a former college professor of his writes him from Los Angeles congratulating him, but the good professor says that he has been unable to buy a copy of the book; his local bookstore had never heard of it. The author, indignant and hurt, sends a copy of this letter to his publisher.

Six months or more after publication the author receives a royalty statement. Only 1904 copies were sold to bookstores! Of these, 402 were returned by bookstores to the publisher, so that the total number of copies sold to the public was 1502. There is an earned royalty of about $750. As the author was paid $2000 in advance, there is no more money due him, and there never will be. There have been no extras, no book club selection, no reprint in paperback, no foreign sales. The author is disgusted. He points out to his wife, to his agent, and to his publisher that he devoted a year or more to the project and has nothing. He does not blame the quality of his book or the whims of popular taste; he puts the blame, mildly upon his agent, strongly upon his publisher. Disgust may prevent him from ever writing another book, or he may be halfway through another book, determined to lick the game.

The above picture is reproduced several thousand times each year. It is a sad picture, sad because of human hopes, but not as sad, not as pointless as the author imagines. Let us suppose the author wrote the book in his spare time, worked an average of ten hours a week for a year. He devoted some 500 hours to researching and writing the book. Most authors unconsciously exaggerate the amount of time they devote to their work; 500 hours would be par for the course with many a book. For this work the author received $4 an hour, a high hourly rate for most people. The author also received certain advantages, impossible to evaluate, and yet of value:

1. The author met some "interesting people" doing his research, made acquaintances, and possibly made a friend.
2. The author broadened his intellectual horizons. He is knowledgeable or a semiexpert on the subject of his book.
3. The author increased his personal prestige. The author's boss heard about the book, perhaps joshed him about it, but secretly thinks the more of him.
4. It is possible that the author will have greater success with another book, his second, third, or fourth. But there is no way of writing the second, third, or fourth until the preceding ones have been completed.

The hard-boiled professional writer making a living at his trade will sneer at the above, and yet most would grudgingly, silently agree. Writing books adds zest to the adventure of living and enriches one's life in other ways than money. The author of this volume has met hundreds of writers who were angry at their publishers because of the small sale of their book. He does not remember ever meeting an author who regretted the weary labor of writing or the excitement or sorrow of publishing a book, even though its sale was microscopic.

Books can be unsuccessful. Books can be best sellers. What is a best seller? Best seller is a loose term. The New York *Times* and various other newspapers get reports from bookstores as to what books sold in the largest quantities during the previous week. From these reports best-seller lists are compiled. The bookstores are inaccurate in their reports, partly because they rarely collate their sales figures week by week, so that their statement of their best-selling books is often a guess, partly because accuracy does not seem to them important. Occasionally a bookstore proprietor will mention a book as doing well because he likes the book or has many copies on hand unsold, or even because of the request of a publisher's salesman. Also, from custom, certain types of books such as gift books and cookbooks are rarely reported as best sellers, regardless of their sales. Even if the bookstore's reporting were accurate, the best-seller list would be an inaccurate record. A book may have an enormous sale in one part of the country, for example, Texas and the Southwest, but be little read elsewhere. Such a book may not be mentioned by enough bookstores to attain the national best-seller list. A book with the same sale spread fairly evenly between all bookstores in the country, and hence reported by a large number, might attain the best-seller list. Likewise, a book that sells ten thousand copies in two weeks might be on the best-seller list for two weeks. A book that sold twenty thousand copies over a period of ten weeks might never reach the best-seller list. Moreover, a book must sell far more copies in November and December to attain best sellerdom than are necessary in July and August. The public rushes to buy books before Christmas. The sales of the top best seller in November may be double the sales of the top best seller in August.

Despite these inaccuracies, the books on the top of the New York *Times* best-seller list are the books being talked about and being sold in large quantities. *The Rise and Fall of the Third Reich* sold 348,107 copies in the bookstore edition from October 1960 to September 1962. It was on the New York *Times* best-seller list for 80 weeks and held the top place for 39 weeks.

What causes a book to be at the top, have an enormous sale, be a best seller? The question should be rephrased. What causes the public to buy a book?

Favorable reviews in themselves do not sell books. Most reviews are favorable. Over and over again books are published, are reviewed prominently, and in glowing terms, and the sale is three or four thousand copies or less. Publicity will not in itself sell a book. In March 1960 a really fine book entitled *This Is Where I Came In* was published. Due to close friendship on the part of the author with the heads of both the Associated Press and the United Press and due to certain timely news items in the book itself, feature articles praising the book ran in nearly every daily paper in America, many of them starting on the front page. The sale of the book was 1718 copies.

If reviews or publicity will not sell a book, advertising cannot be expected to. Publishers have tried advertising over and over again without success. Advertising in itself will never sell a book.

What can a publisher do to sell a book? He can package his product well, go through the publishing motions efficiently and hope for the best. A good title, an effective jacket, a strong sales force, and suitable publicity and advertising will increase the sale of any book. But, in themselves, they will never make any book a best seller. Perhaps a book that has been produced haphazardly and distributed inefficiently will sell 2000 copies whereas, properly packaged and handled, it would have sold 4000 copies. With best sellers the sales ratio between a good publishing job and a poor one is not as great, although the difference in copies sold is much greater. Perhaps a good publishing job can sell 75,000 copies of a book that would otherwise sell 50,000. The publisher's activity by itself never makes a best seller.

But what does make a book sell? The major factor is a book of such a nature that one person who reads it recommends it to another. Mrs. Snooks asks Mrs. Jones, "Have you read *The Rise and Fall of the Third Reich?*" In the case of a best seller this question, with its implied recommendation, is asked by thousands and thousands of people. The publisher must obtain a manuscript of such a nature that it will receive such word-of-mouth recommendation. Then the publisher must get enough people to read the book at the start so that such word-of-mouth recommendation can begin. To the extent that word-of-mouth recommendation exists, advertising will spur it on. Mrs. Snooks has recommended the book to Mrs. Jones. Mrs. Jones forgets to do anything about it. An advertisement reminds and spurs her to go and buy the book. Advertising will not create word-of-mouth recommendation. Once word-of-mouth recommendation fades away, advertising will not revive it. Nothing will sustain a wilting flower. Of course, all of the above is a matter of degree. Word-of-mouth recommendation may occur a few hundred times with a resulting modest sale, or it may occur thousands and thousands of times and result in a best seller. Word-of-mouth recommendation may continue for a year or more, or it may die within a month.

The quality of the book, what is between the first page and the last, is the big factor in a successful sale. The publisher has a limited role. Just as a bad surgeon can save a patient's life and a good surgeon can lose a patient, so it is with publishers. No matter how bad the publisher, a book with the requisite qualities will sell; the best publisher in the country cannot sell a book that readers do not recommend.

Do publishers recognize a best seller when they read the manuscript? In nine cases out of ten a manuscript which ultimately proves to be a best seller is grabbed by the first publisher who is offered it. Stories are continually being circulated about a best seller that was declined in manuscript by a long list of publishers. Usually the manuscript that was declined was inferior. Perhaps, after many declinations, one editor had the wit to see how a poor manuscript could be rewritten so as to be a winner, or perhaps the author saw the troubles and rewrote the manuscript under his own steam. This does not mean that the publisher who accepts a manuscript which ultimately has a large sale recognized it as a sure or even a probable best seller. He recognized it as a good commercial manuscript, one that should sell a few thousand copies minimum, and one that had a chance for the big time.

By publication date the publisher has the reaction of his sales people, of large buyers of books, of the trade papers, of the book clubs, and possibly of the paperback publishers. In four out of five cases he knows that he has either a failure, a book that will earn its way but not sell in large quantities, or a best seller. The trade reaction can be wrong but usually is not. One can almost smell a best seller. The writer of this volume, at publication time, often writes down a figure as to the probable sale of a book. Usually he is quite close to the ultimate sale. In one out of five cases he is wrong. *The Rise and Fall of the Third Reich* was a fifth case.

If an author has an enormous reputation from the sale of his previous books or from his activities in public life, a book by him may be assured of a large sale. If President Kennedy wrote his memoirs commercial failure would be inconceivable. Shirer's next book is almost certain to reach 50,000 readers at a minimum. Louis Nizer's next book is not likely to attain the success of *My Life in Court* but it will have a large sale. Every book is subject to the whims of popular taste. There seems to be a fashion in what people want to read. Linda Christian's memoirs sold 7500 copies. If written and published shortly after the successful *I'll Cry Tomorrow*, the Christian memoirs might have had a large sale. In the fall of 1962, when Linda Christian's memoirs were published, the fashion in sex memoirs seemed to be over. A good disaster book published shortly after the publication of *A Night to Remember* would probably have done much better than the same book would do today. However, what the fashion will be and how long it will run is unpredictable.

Obviously, a publisher who cannot predict a best seller from a manuscript cannot tell an author how to write one or even suggest a winning book-idea. The author of this volume believes that a good book on the glorious decline of England, a book covering England from the First World War until the Suez crisis would be a best seller. If such a book is written and does not have a large sale, there is always an alibi: one can always say that the book was not well enough done. Publishers, agents, teachers of writing, and, above all, authors, cannot fashion a best seller. Often publishers can say no as to a particular manuscript with a great deal of accuracy; never can they say yes, this is a certain best seller, unless the author's name assures yes.

All that can be said is that the best-seller lightning is more likely to strike the writer who has learned his trade, who is alive to the interests and affairs of people, who is shrewd in selecting his book-idea, and who is prepared to do an immense amount of research work. Of course, doing the above cannot guarantee a best seller. It cannot even guarantee a substantial sale. It can guarantee a better sale than would occur without such. A book's sale is always hurt by:

1. Lack of freshness in the book-idea.
2. Skimpy research.
3. Poor organization.
4. Poor writing.

It is always helped by a good book-idea, intense research, good organization, and good writing.

The author of a successful non-fiction book tends to follow a pattern. The author has awakened one fine morning to find himself famous. He is elated. The letters, the telephone calls, the requests for him to speak, to autograph copies, to meet other well-known people, to do this and that keep him pleasantly occupied for several months. All his friends congratulate him. A few even read his book and wonder secretly how he was able to write it. Much as he hoped for success, the rewards in acclaim and in money are far greater than he ever dreamed. If his contracts are properly drawn he is carried financially for two or more years, the length of time depending upon whether there was a book club selection, a big magazine sale, a large paperback reprint deal, or even a motion picture, or perhaps just depending upon how many copies were sold through bookstores.

The above is all fine, but no book remains on the best-seller list forever. Royalties ultimately cease, and the author, if he is to support himself, must continue to write. He researches and writes a second non-fiction book for which he has already received a contract from his publisher at attractive terms. The publisher accepts the new book without waxing overenthusiastic. It is published. Perhaps the second book sells 20,000 copies. Compared to most other books it is a success. Compared to the author's previous book, the best seller, it is an out-and-out failure. Perhaps the success of the previous book has gone to the writer's head a little and, as a result of cockiness and self-assurance, the next book is not done with the volume of research, with the amount of revision and rewriting that went into the previous book. Or, more likely, perhaps the book-idea for his best seller was one which had been with the author for years and had grown upon him, while the book-idea for the latest book never had the same potentialities and was not as carefully thought out and developed.

However, such an author writes a third book and then a fourth, and many after that. Occasionally he takes an article assignment. Due to his book success, magazines will pay him higher prices. Usually he repeats his best-seller experience, although it may not be until the fourth, fifth, or eighth book.

There have been occasions when a writer produced a best seller and then faded into oblivion. In 1943 a journalistic type of book had an enormous sale. Most people of discernment considered it badly organized and badly written. It had a good book-idea (anti-Fascist, anti-Nazi theme) which the author felt strongly about and was driven to write by a great compulsion. The book was widely promoted over the radio by Walter Winchell, who at that time had a large following and could interest people in buying and reading a book. The book-idea attracted the American public and it became a best seller. However, the author had not sufficiently learned his trade as a writer, and his subsequent career has been that of a relative failure. The above is exceptional. The general rule is that a man who has written one best seller will repeat. There is plenty of time. The author referred to will probably follow the general rule and write another successful book.

Authors are apt to think of big successes in terms of the New York *Times* best-seller list. A best seller looms large in the public mind; its importance is exaggerated. There are many books which, because of their nature or because of the way they are sold to the public, never reach the best-seller list. In 1961 Meredith Publishing Company published a book on sewing which has earned the author $20,000 and will earn much more. Elise Miller Davis wrote a book on the cowboy stars Roy Rogers and Dale Evans which sold 72,120 copies and earned over $42,850. Neither book ever reached the best-seller list. A book club may use a book as a bonus to its subscribers, as occurred with an animal book by Mary Baker, and the returns to the author can be large. A magazine like *American Heritage* or *Life* may sell a book by mail to the tune of 100,000 copies or more. Such books do not bring the author the acclaim that arrives if a book is high on the New York *Times* best-seller list, but still there is much remuneration and considerable acclaim.

A few writers, those who have independent means or whose writing income is enormous, do not do all the work themselves. They hire researchers. The purpose is to save the writer's time. Projects in the historical or biographical field are most suitable for this kind of help. Under any circumstances, a writer should prepare his first couple of books without the help of paid researchers. The writer must learn how to organize and handle his own research before he can profitably direct others to help him. Even with paid researchers the writer must do much of the research work himself. Researchers are never essential to success, and many writers believe researchers are of little or no help. Probably nineteen out of twenty writers do all their own research.

Some writers look for collaborators. Eugene Burdick is a popular current example. He wrote *The Ugly American* with Paul Lederer and *Fail Safe* with Harvey Wheeler. James Michener wrote *Rascals in Paradise* with A. Grove Day. In a collaboration both research and writing are divided between two writers.

A handful of writers, instead of looking for a collaborator, run a writing factory in imitation of Alexandre Dumas. They hire other writers to research and write. Usually the head of the factory contributes the ideas, supervises, and polishes the final product.

All of the above is deceiving. Success often branches out in many curious directions. The basis of any one writer's success is extreme personal competence. This is what the writer-in-training should primarily be concerned with.

A book writer has the unique experience of having his own product packaged as his own with the theoretical possibility that it will be sold by the millions and appear in a large number of American homes. No author expects such success, but he hopes for it. Failure after months or even years of effort is not easy to take in one's stride. The odds against any particular non-fiction book having a large sale are enormous. For one thing, on the average twenty-five titles are published every weekday of the year. Of these, some fifty annually obtain an enormous distribution. Seven thousand nine hundred do well or do badly, but not supremely well.

Books can be failures; many are. Books can be successful; more are than authors realize. But the careers of most books and hence most authors are not at the top or at the bottom. Books sell in quantities ranging from under 2000 copies to over 500,000 copies. Half or more of all published books are modest successes, make some money for author and publisher, do not make the author rich or famous, but appreciably add to his income and his prestige. A book on flower arranging will probably have only a modest sale, but the author may be reasonably well paid for her efforts, and acclaim may reach her in the form of numerous requests to speak before garden clubs. The author has become an admired expert in something that women are interested in. Moreover, the large number of writers who make a modest success may always strive for something higher with the next book. There is no ceiling to possible success.

Every writer has three problems that are common in every walk of life but accentuated in the world of the written word. The first problem is for the writer to make himself work. Some writers live in an atmosphere of compulsion. Once they are started, an inner force drives them to research, write, research, write. Winston Churchill in a speech said:

> "Writing a book is an adventure; to begin with it is a toy and an amusement, then it becomes a mistress, and then it becomes a master, and then it becomes a tyrant; and the last phase is just as you are about to be reconciled to your servitude,—you kill the monster and fling him about to the public."

Nearly all writers feel this compulsion occasionally, perhaps when they are on the final chapter of a book. But the average day for most writers is one in which they would like to loaf, do anything but research, organize, write, and rewrite. The writer is more his own boss than most self-employed individuals. A lawyer's clients, a doctor's patients, are pressure forces for work. A writer has only himself to drive himself. Also, the relation between hours of work and income is not crystal clear. If a writer takes a month's vacation each year, he reduces his income by one twelfth, but the one-twelfth reduction in income may not show up in any one year. The reduction in income while there never seems obvious.

Some writers get lazier and lazier, and often, with the help of drink, ruin their lives. The majority learn the art of self-whipping. For fear of the habit of laziness, they may keep elaborate diaries of their daily accomplishments. They force themselves to keep regular hours at their desks, and when their writing seems to go badly they turn to research.

The second problem of the writer is to keep up with the times, keep in tune with the ever changing thoughts, hopes, fears, beliefs, accomplishments, and failures of mankind. This is necessary for the writer's own creativity. The good writer is usually an avid reader, a good and constant listener, ever seeking different types of people. Often he is an assiduous traveler. The writer who plays bridge every Friday, golfs every weekend, sees in rotation the same people, and scarcely leaves his house for a night except at Christmas when he visits his old mother, such a writer is heading for trouble. The successful writer is a dynamo of energy in his work and a constructive loafer in his play, which he continually varies.

The third problem for the book writer is how he shall direct his energies. The article writer is directed by the needs and dictates of magazine editors. The book writer must direct himself.

Most successful writers concentrate on one type of writing: a biographer on biography, a science writer on science, a

William Shirer on international political reporting. There are exceptions. A John Gunther, primarily an international reporter, author of *Inside Africa, Inside Asia, Inside Latin America,* writes a best seller that is an emotion book, a brutal assault on the feelings, *Death Be Not Proud.*

One advantage of concentration is that the author saves time. Research with the previous book helps with the new one. *Inside Africa* may not give the author any facts for *Inside Latin America,* but because of the first book, false lines of investigation are less likely to be followed in the second. Learning how to handle the material in the first book gives the author an approach and makes the handling of the second book easier. Another reason for concentrating one's effort in a particular field is that concentration helps build a name and reputation. Many readers interested by the first book want to read the second because of its similarity of subject matter. A leading science writer develops a following among readers of science. A writer who produces a popular science book, then a travel book, then a biography of a literary figure has to start with each book almost from scratch, and his publisher for each book has to find new readers. The author who wanders around is under a handicap compared to the one who concentrates. Many writers-in-training have a fear of being typed. Most famous writers in previous centuries have been typed. For example, it is hard to imagine Darwin having written a history of Italian art.

None of the above will help a writer to concentrate his energies and decide what he shall write. Here no outsider can help. The writer-in-training should follow and, more important, develop his own field of interest. If the goal is to obtain a large readership, he should probe for what is of concern to others. A writer should not write about what people *should* be interested in; he should write about what they *are* interested in.

Writers are subject to two dangers. Depression and discouragement are danger number one. Egotism and a swelled head are danger number two. These dangers exist in all occupations. But the writer, whose work is so lonely, is peculiarly liable to depression and discouragement, and when he is successful, he receives so much publicity that he is especially vulnerable to the threat of egotism and a swelled head. To help the writer overcome his discouragement is one of the purposes of this volume. Non-fiction writing can be learned. The need and demand for it is continuous and ever growing. The biggest factor in success is to learn one's trade and then indulge in that old-fashioned virtue of hard work over a long and continuous period of time. As for the danger of a swelled head, that only affects the highly successful, and while it is hard to live with, still it is one of life's minor troubles.

SUPPLEMENT

SUPPLEMENT

"New York's New Queen of Fashion" by Jack Alexander, reprinted from *The Saturday Evening Post*
"Atlanta: 1864—A Man's Battle Fought by Boys" by Douglas Kiker, reprinted from *Look*
"A Seat Belt Could Save Your Life" by Tom Mahoney, reprinted from *Reader's Digest*
Outline of "A Seat Belt Could Save Your Life"
Description of The Authors' Guild, The Society of Magazine Writers, and The Society of Author's Representatives
Reprint of pamphlet from The Society of Authors' Representatives
Form contract offered by William Morrow & Company, Inc.
Contract clauses pertaining to author's book royalty

The following three articles, referred to in the text, were picked at random from *The Saturday Evening Post, Look,* and *Reader's Digest* as typical examples of the average popular magazine article. The first, "New York's New Queen of Fashion," is a profile of a current personality who is of interest to women. The second, "Atlanta: 1864—A Man's Battle Fought by Boys," is a routine article dealing with the past. The third, "A Seat Belt Could Save Your Life," is the crusade type of piece.

NEW YORK'S NEW QUEEN OF FASHION

By Jack Alexander

Broke and out of work in 1942, exuberant Pauline Trigère has risen to the top in fashion's hectic, glamorous world.

One of the most engaging intercontinental love affairs of the century thus far has been that of Paris-born Pauline Trigère, now an eminent fashion designer, and the United States of America. Sparked by chance, the affair up to now has enjoyed a successful run of twenty-four years, and it shows no sign of faltering. It got its start when Pauline, her husband, Lazar Radley, a Paris tailor, and other members of the clan, stopped off in Brooklyn early in 1937 to visit relatives. They were en route to Santiago, Chile, where Radley had arranged for a business connection.

On a bitter, blustery January day the Radleys, leaving the rest of their party at the St. George Hotel, took the subway to Manhattan and set out to explore the wonders of the Fifth Avenue shopping area, first from the exposed upper deck of a bus and after that on foot. The young woman kept one hand glued to her small black-satin hat to prevent the gusts from whisking it away. The sharply edged ice on the sidewalks jabbed through the delicate sole of her French shoes and made her wince at each step. She was sniffling and red-nosed; yet the more bedraggled she got, the deeper she felt herself falling in love with America.

What most aroused her affections was the lavish assortment of dresses which were copies of originals by such masters of the *haute couture* as Lanvin, Patou and Molyneux. They were priced at $19.95, a figure which made it possible for a reasonably provident working girl to buy herself a swatch of glamour now and then. Such copies were never available in Paris, as popularization of expensive gowns was frowned upon and only the well-to-do could afford them.

Something about a Saks Fifth Avenue window aroused a sensation of sheer exuberance within the half-frozen *Parisienne*. It depicted a tropical beach scene in which languorous models in skimpy bathing suits lolled stiffly on the sand and a fake sun shed fake actinic rays upon them. The young woman, whose voice is normally husky, expressed the exuberance she felt by letting out a hoarse cheep of delight.

Then, with tears of cold joy flowing down her cheeks, she turned to her husband and said, "You can go to Chile. I am staying."

That torpedoed the South American expedition, and it confronted the wandering troupe—among them the Radleys' two small sons, Pauline's older brother, Robert, and her mother—with a crisis. Its treasury was running low, and out of bald necessity it put its roots down in Manhattan in the form of a ladies' custom-tailoring shop in West 47th Street.

This venture, strangely, was destined to die primarily of volume of business. Through the influence of a friend, a steady stream of well-heeled women, mostly from Washington, moved through the shop. The trouble with them as customers was that they demanded cut-rate prices; and the trouble with the proprietors was they couldn't say no. By the time all of the fittings and alterations had been made, there wasn't much profit left.

Another trouble was a marked difference in styling between the Radleys. Radley favored the traditional French approach. His wife, with professional daring, kept trying to express the free-wheeling American spirit, which was easy to sense, as she had sensed it on Fifth Avenue, but difficult to express by a twist of cloth.

Then, too, there was a constant clashing of temperaments. Pauline was, as she is today, mercurial, lively, voluble, dramatic and unpredictable. Radley was quiet, brooding and scholarly. Early in 1941, when the West 47th Street venture was abandoned, the Radleys separated and were subsequently divorced, with Pauline getting custody of the children and restoration of her maiden name.

Today, two decades later, Pauline Trigère is at the peak of a tirelessly prosecuted career. As Trigère, Inc., she designs every coat, dress or suit that leaves her large *salon* and workshop high up in a Seventh Avenue building that overlooks Manhattan's immense garment industry. For the past five years her annual output in terms of what her productions sell for at retail is estimated at between $2,000,000 and $4,000,000. She has an apartment on Park Avenue and a country place near New Canaan, Connecticut. Her protective elder brother, Robert, functions as her business manager and as her ever-ready cheering section when her self-confidence weakens, as it does intermittently.

On her staff is one of her sons, Jean-Pierre Radley, who is a graduate in business and engineering administration of the Massachusetts Institute of Technology. The other son, Philippe Radley, is at Harvard. A gifted linguist, Philippe is fluent in three or four languages, including Russian. He is now working toward a doctorate in the Slavic languages while, under the Harvard tutorial system, tutoring undergraduates in Russian literature.

Over the years the name of Pauline Trigère has become a power in the American world of high fashion. Its bearer rates indisputedly among the top three designers. That is the considered opinion of the newspaper and magazine fashion critics. Annually the critics bestow a prize upon the designer whose works for the year have embodied the most originality and imagination.

steaks, Miss Trigère began teaching the other guests to stand on their heads. This aroused so much hilarity, especially after some of the guests fell into the swimming pool, that the neighbors complained. The crew of a police car quieted down the guests and departed.

Miss Trigère actually had some competence in the stunt she was trying to teach. Her first act on arising in the morning is to do a headstand for at least five minutes. This is part of a yoga regimen which she has been studying for some years. She feels that it tones up her brain and protects her, to a certain degree, from the tensions of her business. It must, or she would have exploded herself to bits by now.

For some years now Miss Trigère, a medium blonde with greenish blue eyes, has been trying to educate women in the art of clothing themselves effectively. Progress has been slow, and the very thought of this puts her in a waspish mood.

"It is so simple," she says. "America is really an extraordinary country, and American women are very lucky. Charming copies of the best originals designed here and in France and Italy can be bought in the stores for twenty-nine or thirty-nine dollars apiece. They are quite stylish. So the trouble is not one of money. It seems to be more of a kind of lack of adventurousness, as it is expressed so often in the fitting room by the remark, 'but it doesn't do anything for me.' What is a pretty dress supposed to do, tickle the wearer or something? It should, of course, provide an attractive frame for her, so to speak, but she should try to do something for the dress, such as keep her weight somewhere near normal."

As an extreme example of what she has in mind, Miss Trigère recalls a customer whom she "dressed" as the saying goes, during her earliest days in New York. The customer, the wife of a famous industrialist, weighed about 250 pounds. She was always going on a reducing diet—and a few hours later sending out for a banana split. "When I saw the woman coming into our showroom I was furious," says Miss Trigère.

"But looking back now I can see that making her clothes for about four years taught me a lot of things about construction. She was an excellent education for me."

The customer's husband weighed as much as his wife, and he always came to her fittings, which both seemed to enjoy in a loud, hearty way.

"He was 'daddy' and she was 'momma,'" Miss Trigère relates, "and when they laughed you could probably hear them up in Yonkers. They came to me with the standard complaint about nobody being able to slim momma down. I did what I could. Made her abandon the fussy clothes she was wearing and, to start off with, got her into some pale, light-colored wool dresses. She didn't look bad, and she didn't look good. She just looked a little less enormous."

One day momma mentioned that they were taking off for the Coast the next day, with time out for a few hours in Chicago. Miss Trigère, who was not long off the boat from France, had heard of Chicago's lurid gang murders, and she wondered aloud why anyone should go there except under duress.

"Oh, we always drop in at the Palmer House," momma explained. "They serve the most delicious pancakes."

It is an axiom of the high-fashion world that the ideal client is a woman of taste, stylishness and money. Miss Trigère whose originals retail at anywhere from $159 to more than $1000, has a few points to add. In the process of adding them she draws a fairly distinct portrait of what might be termed the Trigère woman. Oddly the Trigère woman closely resembles her creator.

"I work," she says, "for the kind of woman who demands a certain kind of façade. She has a certain carriage; she has to have. She does not hide behind a mink. She is discriminating and she knows the needs of her figure. She is active—I don't mean that she has to ride horses or play golf. What I mean is that she has things in her mind; things to do, a family to take care of, certainly a husband, some responsibility of one kind or another. In short, I try to make intelligent clothes for the intelligent woman. I try to make her pretty and at the same time functional. I don't want her to feel fettered by the fit of her clothes. I myself work a lot and move around a lot, and I can't be bothered with something that is too tight in the armholes or that squeezes my rib cage.

"So many women today squeeze themselves into clothes that are tight, in the belief that this will make them look slimmer. Wrong. The woman who looks slimmer is the one whose clothes allow her to move freely."

Only an innate bounciness kept Pauline Trigère from giving up completely after the failure of the West 47th Street venture. The small disaster aroused her fighting instinct. Both she and her brother Robert retained faith in the excellence of her designing talents. Lacking the capital to exploit them, they got jobs and saved rigidly. Robert hit the road as salesman for a fabrics manufacturer. Pauline went into the employ of the late Hattie Carnegie, as an assistant designer in a loft at 18 East 56th Street. It was one of a cluster of Carnegie designing rooms located in lofts within the orbit of her central *salon*.

This job lasted less than three months. In 1941, after the bombing of Pearl Harbor, purveyors of luxury items, among them Hattie Carnegie, began to retrench. Just before Christmas the handful of girls working in the East 56th Street satellite received their notices and severence pay. Assistant designer Trigère, who had a wry sense of humor, decided that the event deserved a proper celebration. Digging into her purse she bought a bottle of vermouth. All hands drank from the bottle, got a little tiddly, exchanged Christmas greetings, cried and laughed alternately and went home.

For some reason this debacle jolted Pauline harder than its predecessor. Christmas week depressed her, and on the day after New Year's Day, 1942, she went to Boston for an overnight visit with some friends whom she had always found invigorating. She drank just enough of their wine to get a bit high, then went to bed. During the night she had a wondrous dream in which a voice asked, "Why don't you go to work for yourself?" A qualified dream analyst probably would have warned her against taking the dream seriously, as she had nurtured the same idea for some time and, in her dream, she had told herself exactly what she most wanted to hear.

Fortunately no dream analyst butted in, and Pauline returned to New York radiating charm and ambition. At a rate of fifty dollars a month she rented the rear half of the old Hattie Carnegie loft in East 56th Street, and her most recent employer was kind enough to leave behind several sewing machines. But there was little else in the way of equipment, and not a stitch of fabric in the establishment.

Speed being of the essence, as it usually is with Pauline Trigère, she pawned the only jewels she owned to raise emergency working capital. The jewels, a diamond barrette and a pair of diamond clips, were presents from her husband, given to her on the occasions of their boys' births. The transaction gave Pauline a severe emotional twinge, but she had prepared herself for that in advance, and it was soon forgotten amid the struggles she was about to undertake.

Wartime fuel rationing combined with her own power drive gave Pauline Trigère an unusually harsh winter. Because her financial stake was limited, she had to get into production fast. Because she was working alone—designing, cutting, pinning, draping—she had to work every night until midnight. At six o'clock each evening the heat was turned off, as the house was classified as a nonessential factory. The terrazzo floors chilled rapidly, and standing on them for any length of time was painful. Pauline solved this one by wrapping her feet in newspapers. Everything metal that she touched was actively cold. When her fingers became numb, she warmed them on the pressing iron. The elevator was also shut down at six o'clock, which meant climbing four flights to the loft when she returned from supper.

But when March came around, all of that was forgotten.

By that time Pauline had finished a group of eleven dresses. It was scarcely big enough to be referred to as a "collection," as the rather grandiose trade term goes, but it was at least a collection in embryo, and Robert, who had returned to the venture, set out to sell his sister's creations. His first two orders came from Hattie Carnegie and Polly's Gowns, his third from Nan Duskin in Philadelphia. While Pauline was assembling a staff to take care of the orders that were coming in, Robert, traveling by bus for economy's sake, beat the bushes all the way to the West Coast, and Trigère, Inc., was on its way. The main actor in the drama got her jewelry out of hock and never had to pawn it again.

"It never killed anybody to work hard," Miss Trigère says about the ordeal of 1942, "if you have a strong incentive. I had more than one. I happened to love the work I was doing. I wanted recognition in the fashion world. I had to eat. If you want to eat you must first earn money to buy food, you know. I also had to feed my children and send them to school. I had a whole barrelful of incentives. I am often asked to give a talk at some school of design. Always some students ask how one gets to be a successful designer. When I tell them that talent plus decades of hard work is the closest I can come to it, they are incredulous. They do not see why they cannot go directly from school into a big job."

Once when she was on her way to Europe Miss Trigère was stopped by a cigar-smoking character on the promenade deck. He identified himself as a coat manufacturer and said bluntly, "I saw your last collection and was disappointed by the coats. There was only one that made me want to copy it."

This little speech might have caused the coat maker some trouble had he made it in Paris, for he was openly proclaiming himself to be a fashion pirate. In France fashion piracy is punishable by law. In the United States it is legal, and the designers whose works are copies are of two minds about it. Some of their potential market may be taken away by the cheaply made imitations; on the other hand, if nobody wanted to imitate their works, the designers would feel neglected and insulted.

On one memorable occasion Robert Trigère intervened in a particularly flagrant case of piracy and lived to regret it. Pauline had designed an especially striking formal cotton dress. It was expensive to make because the skirt was a series of graduated tucks, and that kind of frippery takes time. The dress was scheduled to be sold for $200 at retail. Before Trigère, Inc., could deliver the dress to its clients, someone had thrown together a batch of hastily made copies and bootlegged them to a department store, which advertised them for $125 apiece. A week later a specialty store offered them at $79.50, at which point Mr. Trigère, a quiet-spoken and gracious gentleman, blew a gasket.

He located the undercover manufacturer, who at the time happened to be in his showroom exhibiting the controversial garment for still another retailer to admire. Trigère grabbed the dress and tore it into strips. The manufacturer tried to prevent this act and in the process got jostled around a little. He sued for $50,000 and settled for $500. The only comment Robert Trigère makes on the case when someone recalls it to mind is, "I lost my temper." Trigère, Inc., was never able to solve the mystery of how the manufacturer brought off his sensational coup.

One reason for Pauline Trigère's swift rise may have been the fact that she was born in a tailoring establishment. The event took place in 1912 in the establishment of Alexander Trigère on the Place Pigalle. Trigère and his wife were Russians who had emigrated from Odessa after the close of the Russo-Japanese war. They lived in rooms in back of the workrooms themselves.

Luck had favored Alexander Trigère in Paris. A handsome man with an impressive dark mustache, he had ten sewing machines in his shop, and most of the time they were humming busily. He himself presided over the cutting tables.

Trigère *père* was what is known in the trade as a contractor —he made up garments for some Paris department stores which provided him with the necessary patterns and materials.

When Pauline was old enough to be allowed in the shop, her father taught her the important art of cutting with frugality. He showed her how a careless cutter wastes cloth, using perhaps three meters where a skilled hand would achieve the same effect with two and a half meters. Life in the back of the tailoring establishment was warm and pleasant, though the quarters were cramped. The Trigères several times a year gave big dinners for friends and relatives. The combination dining-sitting room being too small, the dinners were given in the shop itself, with the dummies and machines tucked away and the long cutting tables spread with white damask.

In the French middle-class manner, Pauline's social life was closely supervised. She went out only with youthful groups or with her parents. They were enthusiastic patrons of the theater, the opera and the concert hall and, luckily, she shared their enthusiasm. Her first solo dates—and the last for many years—were with a young Russian *émigré* whom a friend in Odessa had referred to Trigère with a request that he be taken on as an apprentice.

Trigère had all the apprentices he could use at the time, but he was able to get him apprenticed to another tailor. That might have ended the newcomer's connection with the Trigère family had not Pauline's elder brother, Robert, taken an interest in him. Robert, then studying for an engineering degree, had already begun to assume a protector's role toward his sister, and he saw in the newcomer a good husband for her. He sold the parents on the idea and, when this was accomplished, it was taken for granted that the couple was engaged. The newcomer was, of course, Lazar Radley. Pauline was fifteen when they met. Two years later, when Radley's savings had reached a suitable total, they were married.

This was in 1929, the year the world began to come apart

at the seams. The economic crisis had no immediate effect upon the family business. When, a couple of years later, Papa Trigère died, the business, thereafter run by a family council, was moved into brighter and roomier quarters on the Avenue de l'Opéra. It did come upon some hard days, but it was weathering them when, in the middle of 1936, the Socialists, headed by Léon Blum, took over the reins of government.

To Radley this meant that the liquidation of the small businessman was just around the corner. He carried his ominous point in the family council. By late in December of 1936 the business had been sold and all of the family council, plus two small sons of the Radleys, were on the high seas en route to Chile, by way of the United States.

As was evident later on, Radley had badly misread the French political news. As a result of his error, Chile lost some immigrants of good quality, Radley took an injudicious walk on Fifth Avenue and the United States acquired a lively young woman who was to become a couturière of real distinction.

Miss Trigère is nothing if not dramatic, and she has so arranged her life that in each twenty-four-hour cycle she progresses from an overworked little slavey to a glamour woman or, in local terms, from Seventh Avenue to Park Avenue. Her working costume consists of a sleeveless cotton blouse, wooden clogs and a wide cotton skirt with a big pocket for her shears. She also wears tortoise-shell glasses, for nearsightedness, and a magnetized wristband for carrying pins. With a fury which rarely abates, she rides her staff ragged—and herself too—insisting on nothing less than perfection. In addition to the weight any command carries, Miss Trigère's commands are backed by her reputation as an immensely skilled tailor. She is, for instance, a virtuoso with the shears, and it is not uncommon for her, with only a rough idea in her mind, to cut up an expensive piece of cloth, drape it on a live model and O.K. it immediately for trial production with an assurance that never fails to electrify her employees.

Around eight o'clock in the evening the metamorphosis is well under way. The ex-slavey, clad in one of her more striking numbers, is waiting in her apartment, maybe for Julio Werthein, a wealthy Argentinian and her most frequent escort, to take her to a concert or show; maybe she is waiting for some 8:30 dinner guests. If the latter, Pauline, an amateur cook of vast talents, will have prepared the main dish. The apartment, furnished in the romantic style, drips with crystal, garnet roses and Louis XVI touches. In each room part of the décor consists of an ice bucket with a bottle of champagne in it. "I like the feeling of having luxury about me and champagne ready if I should happen to want some," Miss Trigère explains.

A naturalized American since 1942, Pauline makes one or two trips to France each year to buy fabrics. Every time she arrives in Paris she suffers a twinge of nostalgia, but soon recovers from it.

"I'll love Paris always," she said, on returning from her last voyage. "But honestly, the lively pace of America is so exciting that sometimes I think it was made just for me."

ATLANTA: 1864—A MAN'S BATTLE FOUGHT BY BOYS

Youth slaughtered youth as North and South fought savagely for the possession of Atlanta. Here is the story of the bloody battle that helped to determine the fate of the Confederacy.

By Douglas Kiker

Atlanta was a young man's battle, fought on the shank end of an old, bitter war. About a quarter of the Union soldiers who closed in on "The Gate City of the South" on July 22, 1864, were 19 or younger. Another quarter were no more than 21. And of the 50,000 Confederate defenders of the battered, panic-stricken town, 35,000 were 21 or younger. Scattered through both forces were boys of 13, 14 or 15.

This was no isolated engagement. On that hot July day, the eyes of the world were on Atlanta. Both enemies and friends of the Confederacy knew that the Southern cause would suffer a catastrophe if Atlanta fell.

The city was still a small one in 1864, with only 13,000 population. But it was the most important railroad center of the South and the nerve center of the Confederacy's fragile supply network.

The Union Army's Gen. William Tecumseh Sherman had pushed south toward Atlanta following victory at Chattanooga in the spring. Standing in the way of his well-equipped, well-supplied army of 100,000 men were 60,000 Confederates under wily Gen. Joseph E. Johnston, the gray wolf. Johnston gave way slowly before Sherman's advance. He never challenged him in open battle, but fought delaying, harassing actions whenever the chance came.

By early July, Sherman had forced his way to the outskirts of Atlanta. On July 17, Confederate President Jefferson Davis, convinced that Sherman should never have got that far, replaced Johnston, his old West Point schoolmate, with John Bell Hood, a hot-headed, one-armed, one-legged corps commander who had a reputation as a man who would put his army on the line and fight it.

Hood quickly lived up to his name. Three days after he took command, he attacked Sherman some miles to the northwest of town, in the Battle of Peachtree Creek. He hoped to trap part of the Union Army in the triangle where the creek meets the Chattahoochee River. It was a bold plan, but it brought disastrous results. Hood lost about 4000 men to Sherman's 2500.

That same day—July 20, 1864—the first shell from Union cannon was fired into the city, marking the beginning of a steady, destructive bombardment that was to last more than a month. According to legend, that first shot fell in the downtown section at East Ellis and Ivy Streets and killed a little girl who was out walking with her parents. War had come to Atlanta, and a frightened city realized for the first time the full horror of things to come.

The next night, Hood tried another daring maneuver. He pulled Hardee's Corps off the northern line of defense and sent it on a 14-mile night march, through the town, out to southeast Atlanta, with orders to strike at the exposed left flank of the Union line in a surprise daybreak attack.

But Hardee didn't get into action until nearly noon, and

then he ran straight into a division of the Federal 16th Corps. Fighting immediately broke out, and the Battle of Atlanta was soon joined.

It raged all that day along a seven-mile front as these two superb armies, each totally committed to victory, traded blows.

On that midsummer day, the young slaughtered the young, and the young comforted the young.

HE COMFORTED FRIEND AND FOE

Eddie Evans, a "mere boy," was color bearer for the 24th Mississippi Rifles. When he saw his company break and fall in the face of deadly Union rifle fire, he took a position in an open field only fifty yards from the enemy line. Defiantly, he waved his flag and rallied the men to attack.

On the Union side, 13-year-old Johnny Clem, the famous "Drummer Boy of Shiloh," was carrying dispatches for Maj. Gen. George Thomas, the commander of the Army of the Cumberland. A Minié ball pierced his ear, and his pony was shot from under him.

J. W. Adams, a farm boy whose home was near the battlefield, carried canteens of water to the wounded men who lay under the trees, and took down a letter from one dying Union soldier who wanted his wife to know that he had fought and died honorably.

In Atlanta itself, Mary Erskine, the teen-age daughter of a local judge, worked from morning until night at a hospital on Whitehall Street, helping Dr. Robert Battey operate on the wounded. Dying men lay in rows on the street. Medical supplies were almost exhausted. Mary Erskine ripped her own petticoat and blouse into strips and used the cloth to bind wounds.

Andrew Jackson Neal, a young lieutenant of the Marion Light Artillery, had his horse killed while he was holding its bridle. Of all the thousands joined in battle that afternoon, perhaps the most symbolic was this young man. He had spent the last 75 days of that spring and summer defending the city he was born and raised in. He had fought down through the north Georgia mountains and foothills from the Tennessee line, across the Chattahoochee River, through Peachtree Creek, and now, finally, he faced the Yankees in the streets and on the wooded hills where he once had played as a boy.

In the midst of the bloody battle were boys who had left farms and towns in Ohio and Iowa and Tennessee and Georgia to rush to recruiting stations when war broke out. Minimum-age enlistment laws were never strongly enforced by either side. It was not until March, 1864, that the Union prohibited the enlistment of boys under 16. The Confederacy never did enforce a minimum-age limit. Youngsters in both North and South, anxious to see battle and jealous of slightly older friends already in uniform, frequently lied about their age to obliging recruiting officers. More often than not, the standard was: "If he looks old enough, he is old enough. Sign him." The historian of Ohio's "Sherman Brigade" estimated, for example, that fully 40 per cent of that group was made up of boys under 20.

Surely the youngest and most frightened of all that day were the boys serving with the hastily assembled, ill-equipped Georgia militia. Most of them were stationed within the strongly constructed system of forts and breastworks that encircled Atlanta.

These were the 2500 recruits "from the cradle and the grave" who had been mustered after Georgia's Gov. Joe Brown called for "all persons between the ages of sixteen and sixty" to take up arms, and Mayor James Calhoun, without mentioning age limitations, had ordered "all male citizens capable of bearing arms to report to the marshal of the city, to be organized into companies and armed."

In Atlanta in 1864, the story was told of a father who took his 15-year-old son to a conscription officer in the city and turned him in for the bounty payment offered as incentive. The officer said the boy looked old enough to be drafted without bounty payment, but the father insisted he was three months short of being 16. The officer paid the bounty, and the father gave his son a dollar of it and sent him off to fight.

The regulars of Hood's army called the Georgia militia "Joe Brown's pets," and one caustic, hard-bitten Tennessee infantry private described them this way:

"It beat Forepaugh's double-ringed circus. Everyone was dressed in civilian clothes. A few had double-barreled shotguns, but the majority had umbrellas and walking sticks." They weren't soldiers, certainly, but they stood up pretty well that day, considering their circumstances.

Even the generals were young. Hood was only 33, and without the war would still have been an obscure lieutenant in the old U. S. Army. The Union Army's Maj. Gen. James B. McPherson, Hood's West Point roommate and closest friend, was shot from his horse and killed by Southern skirmishers. He was 36.

The young soldiers led by their youthful officers battled savagely. One Union general said that the day's action had "no parallel during the war" for "impetuosity, splendid abandon and reckless disregard."

When desperate charges ended, opposing troups often found themselves occupying opposite sides of the same running mound of breastworks. This resulted in much hand-to-hand combat. One observer who visited the field just after the battle said he found the bodies of "young boys—the Blue and the Gray—clasped in a fierce embrace. What had passed between them could never be known."

Capt. David P. Conyngham, a Union soldier-correspondent, reported that he came upon a young Union soldier that day "sitting with the head of a dying rebel in his lap." They were brothers who had come to the United States from Germany. The older brother had arrived first and stayed in the North. The younger had followed, wandered south trying to locate him and was conscripted into the Confederate Army in Macon, Ga. Captain Conyngham said the Union soldier held his younger brother, comforted him and talked with him of their home and family in Germany until the boy died in his arms.

But perhaps the most revealing comment of all on the battle came from 20-year-old Charles Harding Cox of the 70th Indiana Regiment, who wrote his mother in suspended horror. "We fought the battle of the campaign, and it was a fair fight. I have nothing strange to write."

Hood lost 8000 men that day; Sherman, 3700. When darkness came, Hood withdrew inside Atlanta's defenses. He tried one more counterthrust, which was smashed at Ezra Church, and then dug in for a grim defensive stand. Up moved heavy Union siege guns to hammer Atlanta day and night. Hood was surely pressed as Sherman extended his lines south to cut the vital railroad to Mobile and Macon. But every Union thrust was parried. Atlanta held on as the hot August days dragged by.

On the night of August 27, patrols reported that Union troops were withdrawing from their trenches. This news sent Hood leaping to his feet. Confederate cavalry raids must have cut Sherman's supply lines and forced him to fall back or starve. "We've won," shouted Hood. The church bells of Atlanta pealed, and a special train brought people from Macon for a victory ball. But in the midst of festivities, officers and their ladies heard the growl of guns. Sherman had boldly cut loose from his supply lines and circled far to the south of Atlanta. His only rail line smashed, his troops mauled by Sherman's all-out attack, Hood withdrew from the city on September 1, 1864. Sherman wired President Lincoln: "Atlanta is ours and fairly won."

During that month-long siege, Lieutenant Neal saw his home town gradually destroyed. On August 3, he wrote his sister Ella: "In some parts of town every house has been struck a dozen times. I see two balls have gone into our house, one in Bud James's room and one in the parlor." Less than a week later, he was killed in action, and a vesper service was held in his memory at Trinity Methodist Church. As the final ironic note, when Sherman finally occupied Atlanta, he chose Neal's home for his headquarters.

The war destroyed one Atlanta, but resulted in the birth of a new, greater city.

Today, it is still possible to dig around and find rusted rifle barrels, Minié balls that missed their mark and, occasionally, brass belt buckles and dented canteens. There are a few markers, too, and many graves, but all the battle lines, the breastworks, the fortifications—these are gone. It is as if Atlanta has purposely tried to obliterate all the evidences of that bitter summer. The city hall now stands on the site of Andy Neal's old home, and expressways and housing projects cover the hills and bottomlands where once thousands of men perished.

The quarrel is done, the issue settled, the fierce sorrows banished. After all, who is to mourn a man—or a way of life—a century dead? The old makes way for the new, and even the bitterest of hatreds dissolve eventually in liquid time.

A SEAT BELT COULD SAVE YOUR LIFE

This simple yet proven device might mean the difference between life and death on the highway. Consider the evidence.

Condensed from *Traffic Safety*

By Tom Mahoney

As a couple drove an elderly woman home from church in Dallas, Texas, a few months ago, another car crashed into theirs at an intersection. It was a minor accident to the cars: one was barely moving, the other was within the speed limit. Neither overturned. But the elderly woman in the back seat was thrown out on the pavement and fatally hurt.

I remember this well. She was my mother.

A few days later two young men in a sports car failed to negotiate a sharp turn on the scenic highway near San Simeon, Calif. The car hurtled into the air and rolled over and over for 200 feet down a 70-percent grade toward the beach. The occupants walked away from the wrecked vehicle with only slight injuries.

What made the life-and-death difference between the two accidents was the use of seat belts such as air passengers fasten when planes take off or land. My mother had none, but the men in the sports car wore belts and, according to the California Highway Patrol, owe their lives to them.

In any collision, an automobile is stopped suddenly but the people inside, unless restrained in some way, keep going—smashing into some part of the interior or, worse, being thrown out. The risk of serious injury or death is five times greater for the person who is ejected than for the person who stays inside a car in an accident. Seat belts, properly installed and worn, prevent this ejection. They cost only $10 to $17 each.

Years of research at Cornell University, at the University of California and elsewhere, and analysis of the accident records of 22 states have confirmed the usefulness of ordinary lap-type belts. A booklet published by the National Safety Council in coöperation with the U. S. Department of Health, Education and Welfare and the American Medical Assn. sums up the data: "An immense amount of scientific research proves that the automotive seat belt is the most effective single item of protective equipment available to reduce the toll of traffic injuries and deaths.

Investigators calculate that 30 to 60 percent of the 30,000 Americans killed annually in automobiles could be saved by seat belts. None of the 442 motorists killed last Fourth of July wore belts. On the other hand a Cornell study of 712 seat belts worn in accidents found that 701 had functioned properly; of the 11 failures nine were due to faulty installation.

Despite this impressive evidence, the public has been slow to accept safety belts. Factory-installed belts were offered as early as 1949 by Nash, predecessor of American Motors. All the major car manufacturers promoted belts in their 1956 models. Again the public was apathetic. Even today only about two cars in 100 have belts and many drivers of cars so equipped do not wear the belts with any regularity.

All U.S. automobile manufacturers now agree on the merits of seat belts. If a substantial number of new car buyers ask for them, automobile-company executives predict belts will become standard equipment on cars. (General Motors is delivering its 1961 Corvette with upholstery-matching belts.) In the meantime, all offer belts as optional equipment.

All the major companies are putting seat belts into cars loaned to high schools for driver-training programs. The Army recommended the use of seat belts after discovering during the Korean War that it was losing more men in automobile accidents than in battle. State police cars in 32 states now have belts. The U. S. Forest Service has used belts in its vehicles since 1954. "Our folks say the belts lessen fatigue on long trips," Seth Jackson, safety officer of the agency, told a Safety Council symposium last October.

Dr. Horace E. Campbell, chairman of the Colorado Medical Society's safety committee, believes that legislation is needed requiring all cars to be equipped with belts. Motorists, he says, should not be given the choice of not having them "any more than they are given the choice of buying uninspected meat." Those who agree point out that automobile accidents are a leading cause of death between the ages of 15 and 25, and that such legislation would merely make automobiles subject to the sort of safety regulations to which ships, airplanes and trains have been subject for decades. In New York, State Senator Edward J. Speno is asking the state legislature to make seat belt attachment points mandatory in all new cars sold in the state after June 30, 1962. Similar legislation has been introduced in Connecticut and Illinois.

Insurance companies have led in putting belts into company automobiles and in encouraging employees to buy them for their own cars. The "America Fore" group of insurance companies had an average of 1.5 fieldmen killed each year before putting belts into its 1429 company-owned cars in 1955. Since then, with more cars going more miles, the company has had only one fatality, and he was sitting on his seat belt.

But the most effective evangelists for seat belts are users who have escaped from serious accidents with little or no injury. Charles Pulse, of the Northern Illinois Gas Co. at Evanston, Ill., was riding along Highway 53 when a car in a collision ahead of him bounced against his car and rolled it over, crushing one side. "When the car came to a stop I was hanging upside down from my seat belt," he says. "Walking away from that wreck with hardly a scratch convinced me. Now I won't drive around the corner without having the belt fastened."

A similar crusader for seat belts is John Fitch, the American sports car driver, who escaped with nothing more than bruises when his car went out of control at 140 miles an hour and rolled end-over-end at a racetrack in Rheims, France. Seat belts can prevent injury on city streets as well. The car in which a friend of mine and his family were driving one night last summer crashed into an unlighted stalled car in the heart of New York City. Those in the rear seat with no belts suffered broken bones but those wearing belts in the front seat were unhurt.

Probably the most dramatic illustration of the value of safety harness was provided last September by the British racing driver, Donald Campbell. While speeding at better than 300 miles an hour on the Bonneville Salt Flats in Utah, his Bluebird II was hit by crosswinds. The machine hurtled through the air for 300 yards, rolled over three times and slid for another 80 yards. Yet Campbell, held in place by his belt and shoulder harness, suffered only a hairline skull fracture as his head struck the cockpit. He arrived at the hospital at the same time as a woman whose car, going 45 miles an hour, had hit a soft shoulder on the road. She broke her leg, pelvis and shoulder.

Sir Donald's experience proved, he said, "that if man can survive a 300-m.p.h. crash, broken bodies are quite unnecessary at lesser highway speeds."

The following outline of "A Seat Belt Could Save Your Life" was prepared not by the author of the article but by the author of this volume:

1. Opening
   (a) Account of fatal accident of author's mother.
   (b) Account of two young men's accident.
2. Theme. Seat belts saved second couple.
3. Argument. Why seat belts save lives.
4. Discussion of public apathy.
5. Discussion of possibilities of legislation.
6. Further examples of how seat belts save lives.
7. Donald Campbell's experience in relation to an experience of another car and driver.
8. Ending. Echo of theme.

Writers-in-training can profit by studying a dozen popular magazine articles, and preparing as a training lesson their own outlines of such articles.

WRITERS' ORGANIZATIONS

Every author should join and give his active support to at least one trade association. The following two are most likely to be of interest to general non-fiction writers. For up-to-date information as to activities, membership requirements, and dues, a letter should be addressed to the secretary.

THE AUTHORS' GUILD
6 East 39th Street
New York 16, N.Y.

This is the largest, oldest, and best-known writers' organization that concerns itself with the improvement of the writing trade. The membership is over 2000. Requirements for membership are loose. Usually the publication of a book or of a short piece of any nature in a magazine of general circulation is sufficient. Dues in 1963 were $25.

THE SOCIETY OF MAGAZINE WRITERS
54 West 40th Street
New York 36, N.Y.

This organization consists of professional non-fiction writers, chiefly article writers. Membership about 200. Requirements for membership: six articles sold to major national magazines in the preceding twelve months; or a non-fiction

WHAT IS A LITERARY AGENT?

A literary agent is an author's business representative. He is responsible for all business and many other matters relative to the writer's total literary output.

What an Author's Representative Can Do for Him

An agent's functions vary in emphasis with the needs of each individual author.

The agent agrees to offer for sale such manuscripts as he believes to be publishable.

He may or may not offer editorial advice on form or content before sending the material out.

He selects the markets which seem to him best suited for the material. In the event of a sale, he negotiates the terms. He collects the monies due, deducts his commission, and forwards the balance to the author. He then handles any other rights in the literary property which he has reserved for the author after the initial sale.

Since the market for good writing is world-wide, there are literary agents in all principal publishing centers. American literary agents maintain working relationships with agents abroad, through whom the work of their clients is offered in all appropriate markets. A literary agency is therefore essentially a service organization for the systematic marketing of literary properties wherever they can be sold.

Some agencies handle an author's work in all fields, including publishing, motion pictures, radio and television. Other agents, specializing in literary material only, work in close association with agencies that handle properties for theatre, the motion pictures, radio and television. On no occasion does their combined fee exceed ten percent for domestic sales.

The agent may be delegated by the author to act for him in his absence in signing contracts and performing similar functions pertaining to his work. An agent protects the author from petty annoyances and takes care of many details which must be promptly and properly handled.

All agents prefer that authors query before sending in manuscripts, describing their work as succinctly as possible. In some instances, the agent queried may suggest a colleague whose special fields of interest better qualify him for dealing with the particular work. Or, if the agent is, at the moment, overloaded with work, he can let the author know, and thus avoid delay.

What an Agent Cannot Be Expected To Do

An agent is not a miracle worker. He cannot sell an unsaleable manuscript—he can only find the best markets and the best terms for a saleable one.

An agent is not an instructor in writing. He cannot afford the time to give detailed critical help to authors whose work has not reached a professional level.

An agent is not a rewrite man. He can direct an author to reputable people when he thinks the material warrants it, but he cannot be expected to do more than minor editing of manuscripts himself.

Standard Practice of an Agent

1. He takes ten per cent commission on domestic sales and up to twenty per cent on foreign sales.
2. He pays out the author's share of monies promptly after receipt.
3. He charges the author with no expense incurred by the normal operation of his office, such as postage

or local phone calls. He does charge the author for such things as copyright fees, manuscript retyping fees incurred at the author's request, copies of books for submission overseas.

4. He does not advertise his services.
5. Some agents may charge a reading fee for unsolicited material, but refund this in the event of acceptance of the material.

How To Find a Good Literary Agent

An agent should be chosen as carefully as a doctor or a lawyer. Any of the following will supply a list of reputable agents:

1. The Authors' Guild of America, 6 East 39th Street, New York.
2. Any nationally known book publisher.
3. Any national magazine.

In 1928, a group of literary agents organized the Society of Authors' Representatives, the address of which is Room 1604, 52 Vanderbilt Avenue, New York, N.Y. This is a voluntary group of agents who subscribe to the ethical practices listed above. Following is a list of the membership of the Society:

American Play Company, Inc.
52 Vanderbilt Ave.
New York, N.Y.

Ashley-Steiner, Inc.
555 Madison Ave.
New York, N.Y.

Lurton Blassingame
10 East 43 St.
New York, N.Y.

Brandt and Brandt
101 Park Ave.
New York, N.Y.

Brandt & Brandt Dramatic Dept.
101 Park Ave.
New York, N.Y.

Curtis Brown, Ltd.
575 Madison Ave.
New York, N.Y.

James Brown Associates, Inc.
22 East 60 St.
New York, N.Y.

Maurice Crain, Inc.
18 East 41 St.
New York, N.Y.

John Tiffany Elliott
341 Madison Ave.
New York, N.Y.

Ann Elmo Agency, Inc.
545 Fifth Ave.
New York, N.Y.

Frieda Fishbein
353 West 57 St.
New York, N.Y.

Samuel French, Inc.
25 West 45 St.
New York, N.Y.

Miss Blanche C. Gregory
366 Madison Ave.
New York, N.Y.

Franz J. Horch Associates
325 East 57 St.
New York, N.Y.

Nannine Joseph
200 West 54 St.
New York, N.Y.

Lucy Kroll Agency
119 West 57 St.
New York, N.Y.

Littauer & Wilkinson, Inc.
500 Fifth Ave.
New York, N.Y.

The Sterling Lord Agency
75 East 55 St.
New York, N.Y.

Harold Matson Company
30 Rockefeller Plaza
New York, N.Y.

Monica McCall, Inc.
667 Madison Ave.
New York, N.Y.

McIntosh, McKee & Dodds
30 East 60 St.
New York, N.Y.

McIntosh & Otis, Inc.
18 East 41 St.
New York, N.Y.

William Morris Agency, Inc.
1740 Broadway
New York, N.Y.

Harold Ober Associates, Inc.
40 East 49 St.
New York, N.Y.

Edmond Pauker
1639 Broadway
New York, N.Y.

Paul R. Reynolds & Son
599 Fifth Ave.
New York, N.Y.

Virginia Rice
145 West 58 St.
New York, N.Y.

Flora Roberts, Inc.
22 East 60 St.
New York, N.Y.

Marie Rodell and Joan Daves, Inc.
15 East 48 St.
New York, N.Y.

Russell & Volkening, Inc.
551 Fifth Ave.
New York, N.Y.

Leah Salisbury
234 West 44 St.
New York, N.Y.

John Schaffner
896 Third Ave.
New York, N.Y.

Constance Smith Associates
119 West 57 St.
New York, N.Y.

Tams-Witmark Music Library, Inc.
115 West 45 St.
New York, N.Y.

Annie Laurie Williams
18 East 41 St.
New York, N.Y.

Willis Kingsley Wing
24 East 38 St.
New York, N.Y.

Following is the form contract proffered by William Morrow & Company, Inc., when they accept a manuscript for publication. This, in the opinion of the author of this volume, is one of the best form contracts proffered by any publisher.

AGREEMENT, made this day of , 19 , between

(hereinafter referred to as "the Author," or, if more than one, "Author" is hereinafter used collectively), and WILLIAM MORROW AND COMPANY, Inc. of New York, New York (hereinafter referred to as "Morrow").
WITNESSETH: WHEREAS, the Author has written or is engaged in writing a work

(hereinafter called "the Work").

NOW, THEREFORE, IT IS AGREED AS FOLLOWS:

AUTHOR'S WARRANTY

FIRST: The Author represents and warrants that he is the sole Author and proprietor of the Work, and has sole and exclusive right to dispose of the same; that the Work has not heretofore been published in book form, that it contains nothing of a scandalous, libelous, injurious or unlawful nature, and that neither the Work nor the title will infringe upon any proprietary right at common law or upon any statutory copyright.

RIGHTS ASSIGNED AND LICENSED

SECOND: The Author hereby assigns to Morrow the following rights in the Work:

a. The sole and exclusive right to print, publish and to market in book form during the whole term of its copyright and all renewals thereof in the United States of America (hereinafter referred to as U.S.A.) and its possessions, in the Philippine Islands, and the Dominion of Canada, and to license others to do so.

b. The sole and exclusive right to license reprint publishers to publish and sell reprint or cheap editions in the territory specified in the preceding paragraph.

c. All rights of dramatization, motion picture rights (including sound and talking motion picture rights), of transmission and reproduction by radio and television in the U.S.A., its possessions and in all foreign countries.

d. With the exception of such rights as may necessarily have been included in a sale by the Author of first serial rights for publication of the Work prior to publication in book form, the sole and exclusive right to license the following subsidiary rights for use, following book publication, in the U.S.A., its possessions, in the Philippine Islands, in Canada and elsewhere in the English language throughout the world with the exception of the British Empire other than Canada: book selection, periodical selection, abridgment or condensation, digest, second serial, and syndication.

e. The sole and exclusive right to license Braille transcriptions, microfilm, recorded readings, and visual projections of the Work as a book, by means of mechanics, light, electricity, or other medium known or to be known, in the territories specified in licenses granted in paragraphs a and g of this section, and similar but non-exclusive rights in territory specified in paragraph f of this section, but such rights shall be exclusive of all dramatic, motion picture, radio and television rights or promotional use of material incidental thereto.

f. The non-exclusive rights to sell copies of any American edition thoughout the world except in the British Empire and to license others to do so.

g. The sole and exclusive right to grant licenses for publication in whole or in part in the English language in foreign countries, for translations into foreign languages and publication of such translations, and for the exercise of any of the other rights enumerated in the foregoing paragraphs, in any foreign country.

DELIVERY OF MANUSCRIPT, ETC.

THIRD: The Author agrees:

a. To deliver to Morrow on or before a manuscript of the Work, not less than words and not more than words in length, in its final form complete and ready for the press. If the Author does not deliver the manuscript as agreed, Morrow shall not be bound by the time limit for publication specified under FOURTH b, and if within month after written notice from Morrow to the Author or his representative, the Author fails to deliver the same, Morrow shall have the option of terminating this agreement and recovering from the Author any amounts which it may have advanced on account.

b. To read, revise and correct and return promptly all proof sheets of the Work; to pay all charges in excess of 10% of the cost of composition for alterations which he makes in proof after the type has been set up in strict conformity with the manuscript, and likewise to pay in full for any corrections in the plates required or which are necessary for the correction of actual errors (excluding printer's errors) after the plates have been made in conformity with the last proof as corrected by the Author, it being understood that these charges, if any, against the Author will be charged against the Author's account, except that if Morrow so requests, payment will be made in cash. It is understood that Morrow will inform the Author of the amount of any excess proof correction charges within one month after receipt of the printer's bill. In the absence of instructions to the contrary, the Author authorizes Morrow to make the manuscript of the said Work conform to its standard style in punctuation, spelling, capitalization, and usage.

c. To supply photographs, drawings, charts, and index necessary to the completion of the Work, and if the Author fails to do so within such time as not to delay publication of the Work, Morrow shall supply the same and shall charge the cost thereof against any sums accruing to the Author under this agreement.

RENEWAL OF COPYRIGHT

d. To take or cause to be taken, as provided by law, all necessary steps to effect renewals of copyright on the expiration of the term thereof and to grant and assign the same or the rights under the same as specified in this contract to Morrow on the same conditions as for the original copyright term. In the event that the present copyright law of the U.S.A. or of any other country where the Work is or may hereafter be protected by copyright, shall be amended or changed or a new copyright law enacted so that the term of copyright is extended or enlarged, Morrow shall forthwith and automatically become entitled to all the rights hereby conveyed, granted and assigned to Morrow for such extended or enlarged term.

OTHER PUBLICATION

e. Not to permit the Work to be published prior to book publication except as a series—i.e. in parts or installments three or more in number —without the written consent of Morrow. When such consent is granted per cent of the proceeds from such publication shall be paid to or retained by Morrow.

f. In case the Work is one of non-fiction, not to publish or permit to be published, during the period the Work is in print, any similar material in book or pamphlet form that will conflict with the sale of the Work, without Morrow's written consent.

g. To notify Morrow promptly of any arrangement made for publication of said Work in whole or in part in any language which would precede book publication by Morrow in the U.S.A. and to provide Morrow at its request with the documents necessary to provide proper copyright protection and to discharge all legal obligations relating to publication in the U.S.A.; and to deliver or cause to be delivered to Morrow, upon its request, 2 complete copies of any edition of said Work, or 2 complete copies of any periodical or newspaper containing a part or all of said Work, which may be published in any language without the U.S.A. prior to the book publication contemplated under this agreement and said copies shall be accompanied by a written notice of the date or dates of the publication thereof. Said copies and said notice shall be delivered to Morrow not later than 6 weeks after such prior publication of the material contained in said copies.

LIBEL

h. To hold harmless and indemnify Morrow against any suit, claim, demand, recovery or expense of any nature whatsoever arising from any claims of infringement of copyright or proprietary right, or claims of libel, or claims based upon or arising out of any matter or thing contained in said Work, and, bearing all costs, to protect and defend the Work from any such adverse claim, provided the claim is finally decided adversely to Morrow in a court of competent jurisdiction, and to pay any judgment that may be awarded against Morrow.

Except in the case of a claim of plagiarism, compromise of which might reflect on the Author's integrity, Morrow shall have sole discretion in determining whether or not to compromise any such claim or suit brought against them. If Morrow considers such an offer of compromise satisfactory, it will so notify the Author, advising him what his obligation, if any, under the compromise would be. If the Author consents to such compromise, Morrow shall pay the first $500., the Author shall pay the second $500. and costs thereafter shall be equally divided between the Author and Morrow. Should the Author disapprove of the settlement proposed, unless such claim of plagiarism is involved, Morrow may either compromise the said claim at its own expense, or permit the said suit to proceed to trial, in which event the Author shall be liable for all fees, costs and expenses, except for attorney's fees and expenses up to date on which he was advised of the proposed compromise, as to which he shall be liable only to the extent set forth in the preceding paragraph.

If during the life of this agreement Morrow shall believe that the copyright or some proprietary right to said Work is being infringed or injured by the act of another, Morrow shall give written notice to the Author. If, after conference, Morrow and the Author shall proceed jointly, then the costs and recovery arising out of said prosecution shall be shared equally. If no agreement is reached for joint action, either party may proceed as he shall see fit, bearing all costs incidental thereto and enjoying all of the benefits arising therefrom. And if either party shall decline to proceed, he shall, upon being indemnified against all costs connected with said proceeding, execute all instruments necessary or convenient to permit the other party to proceed in his own name, at his own cost, and for his own benefit.

to 6% of the retail price; on editions priced at less than $1.00, an amount equal to 4% of the retail price on each copy sold, less returns; an amount equal to 50% of all net amounts received as royalty from others licensed to publish and sell reprint or cheap editions.

The royalty on all copies of the Work in the regular edition remaining unsold in the hands of booksellers at the time of publication of any cheap or reprint edition shall be adjusted to conform to the same terms as for such reprint edition, provided that Morrow makes rebates or credits on such copies to enable booksellers to retail such copies at the price of the reprint edition. Any overstock of the regular edition sold as a remainder to the reprint publisher at or below manufacturing costs shall not be subject to royalty.

VI. In any 6 months' royalty period following that of publication, if the sales of the Work do not exceed 500 copies and provided always that such sales are from a reprinting of   copies or less, 75% of the rate of royalty stated first in FOURTH c.I., computed on such semi-annual sales of 500 copies or less, this reduction in royalty being made by reason of the high cost of manufacture of such small reprintings, and a concession by the Author for the purpose of keeping the Work in print.

VII. In the event of special editions being licensed for a definite sum or royalty to any book club or like organization, an amount equal to 50% of the amount received.

VIII. Although no payment shall be made by Morrow when permission is given gratuitously for the publication of extracts from said Work to benefit the sale thereof, an amount equal to 50% of all amounts received from the sale of second serial, digest and all other rights stipulated under SECOND d and e.

IX. From rights of dramatization, or motion picture rights, or radio, television, and all other rights stipulated in SECOND c, an amount equal to   per cent of net amounts received after deduction of agent's fee, if any.

X. In the event of a sale of rights in England or other foreign countries or of translation rights an amount equal to   per cent of the amounts received for such rights after deduction of agent's fee and taxes withheld abroad, if any. If, however, Morrow furnishes sheets or bound copies of the Work for foreign publication, the production cost, including an allocable part of composition and plate amortization, shall be deducted from the amount received and Morrow shall pay the Author an amount equal to one-half of the balance.

XI. As an advance against and on account of all monies accruing to the Author under this agreement:

AUTHOR'S COPIES

d. To give to the Author 10 copies of said Work in the original edition and 3 copies of every reprint edition and to sell to the Author further copies for personal use and not for resale at 60% of the retail price.

ACCOUNTING AND SETTLEMENT

e. For 4 years following publication to submit semi-annual statements of sales as of December 31 and June 30 on April 1 and October 1, respectively, and to pay to the Author the amounts due him 30 days later (May 1 and November 1). After 4 years Morrow reserves the right to render annual statements as of December 31 on April 1 should the sale of the Work be less than 200 copies per year. Whenever the annual sales fall below 50 copies, and after notification of the fact to the Author, no accounting shall be made until the next annual settlement date after such sales aggregate 50 copies.

f. To report promptly to the Author or his representative any contracts entered into for the sale of any rights granted or licensed under SECOND b, c, d, e, or g whenever the Author's shares of the guaranteed payment or royalty is to be $100. or more. Contracts may be examined by the Author or his representative at the Morrow office, but copies will be furnished only upon written request.

GENERAL CONDITIONS

FIFTH: It is mutually understood and agreed:

a. That if the Author has received any overpayment of royalties as a result of returns, or rebates on sales in connection with a cheap edition, Morrow may deduct the amount of this overpayment from any future earnings on other books of the Author which may be published by Morrow, it being understood, however, that the term "overpayment" does not apply to an unearned advance.

b. If, in the opinion of Morrow, any manuscript delivered under this agreement shall require correction or retyping as proper preparation for the press, then Morrow shall notify the Author, and if the Work has not been announced for publication within 4 months after the date of delivery of the manuscript, the Author shall have 30 days after the receipt of such notice in which to edit and deliver a corrected manuscript. Upon his failure to do so, Morrow shall have the right to cause said corrections to be made at the expense of the Author. If the Work has been announced for publication within 4 months after the date of delivery of the manuscript, should the Author not be immediately available, and, if delay would cause postponement of publication, Morrow may proceed at once to cause said corrections to be made at the expense of the Author. Any such charges against the Author's account, however, shall be fair and reasonable.

c. One year after publication or any time thereafter if Morrow has an overstock of the Work, after notification by mail to the Author or his representative, the Author shall have the right for 30 days to purchase for cash any part of said overstock at 25% of the catalogue price. If he fails to do so, Morrow shall have the right to dispose of said overstock as it may see fit, subject to royalties hereinbefore specified, provided it keeps on hand a stock adequate for any reasonable demand for a further two year period in the case of fiction, or four year period in the case of non-fiction or juveniles.

d. If at any time during the continuance of this agreement Morrow elects to discontinue permanently the publication of said Work it shall notify the Author in writing, mailed to his last known address, whereupon the Author, upon payment to Morrow of any outstanding indebtedness, may if he so desires terminate this agreement forthwith, recovering all rights granted to Morrow. The Author also shall have a 30 day option to buy for cash all copies on hand at the cost of manufacture and any existing electrotypes, plates, engravings and dies at one-third of their cost to Morrow including composition. If the Author fails to exercise such option, Morrow may dispose of such material as it sees fit without any payment or any other obligation whatsoever to the Author except that Morrow will, upon request, notify the Author of the disposition.

e. If all editions of the said Work be out of print and there has been no reprint or cheap edition contracted for or optioned by Morrow, and if within 30 days after written demand by the Author, or his representatives, Morrow does not agree to provide within 6 months adequate stock to meet the normal demand for the Work or to arrange for a reprint edition within 6 months, then upon repayment of any unearned advance, overpayment of royalties, or other sums due Morrow, this agreement shall forthwith terminate and all rights in the Work shall revert to the Author, who shall also have the right for a period of 30 days thereafter to buy the electrotypes, plates, engravings and dies, if any, at one-third their cost to Morrow including composition. Upon payment therefor and of any other amounts due Morrow hereunder, this agreement shall forthwith terminate and all rights in the Work shall revert to the Author.

f. Notwithstanding rights granted Morrow under SECOND d, the Author expressly reserves, for the exploitation of motion pictures based upon said book or dramatizations, the rights to publish in any and all forms, but not exceeding 7,500 words in length, excerpts, summaries, novelizations and dramatizations of the Work.

g. The Author or his authorized representative shall have the right, upon written request, to examine the books of account of Morrow insofar as they relate to the said Work, which examination shall be at the cost of the Author unless errors of accounting amounting to 5% or more of the total sums paid to the Author shall be found to his disadvantage, in which case the cost shall be paid by Morrow.

PUBLISHER'S LIABILITY

SIXTH: Morrow is not an insurer of manuscripts, drawings or other property of the Author placed in possession by him, and it shall be liable for any loss or damage thereto only in the event of gross negligence on its part or that of its employees. Morrow shall not be required to carry insurance of any kind for the benefit of the Author.

BANKRUPTCY

SEVENTH: In the case of bankruptcy or liquidation of Morrow, for any cause whatever, provided Morrow is not in default for 30 days or more on any payments due the Author, the Author shall have an option for 90 days to buy back the rights of publication, also plates, bound copies and sheets at their fair market value, to be determined promptly by agreement or arbitration, and thereupon this agreement shall terminate. In case Morrow is in 30 day default to the Author, the above option shall be broadened to permit recovery of publication rights without payment for such rights upon purchase by the Author of plates, bound copies, and sheets.

EIGHTH: The right to receive payment hereunder may be assigned by the Author, but the other obligations imposed upon him are personal and non-assignable.

ARBITRATION

NINTH: Any controversy or claim arising out of or relating to this agreement, or the breach thereof, shall be settled by arbitration, in accordance with the Rules, then obtaining, of the American Arbitration Association in the City of New York, and judgment upon the award rendered may be entered in any Court having jurisdiction thereof.

TENTH: Descriptive words and statements used in the margin of this contract to describe the contents of certain paragraphs thereof are not to be deemed a part of the contract or as a representation as to the contents thereof. Each party agrees that he has read this entire agreement and understands the contents thereof.

IN WITNESS WHEREOF, the parties hereto have signed and sealed this agreement at New York, New York, in triplicate, the day and year first above written.

In the presence of:
as to the author

_______________________ _______________________ (L. S.)

WILLIAM MORROW AND COMPANY, Inc.

as to William Morrow and Company, Inc.

_______________________ By _______________________ (L. S.)

CLAUSES IN PUBLISHER'S CONTRACTS THAT MODIFY SPECIFIED ROYALTY

The following clauses reprinted from the form contract of Henry Regnery Company are typical of many publishers' form contracts:

The publisher agrees except as otherwise is provided to pay the author royalties on all copies sold, as follows: 10% of the catalogue retail price on all copies sold up to and including fifteen thousand (15,000) copies; fifteen per cent (15%) on all copies sold thereafter.

With the following exceptions:

(a) when in its judgment it shall be necessary or advisable, the publisher may sell at a discount of fifty per cent (50%) or more; each such sale shall be accounted for separately, and shall not be included in sales totals. When copies are sold at a discount of fifty per cent (50%) or more, a ten percent (10%) royalty shall be paid on the net amount actually received by the publisher.

The second paragraph above, paragraph (a), modifies the first paragraph. Under the first paragraph the publisher of a book selling to the public at $4, when the royalty rate is 10 percent, would pay the author a royalty of $.40 on each copy sold. Let us assume that the publisher gives the book buyer a 47 percent discount, in other words, permits the book buyer to retain 47 percent of what the customer ultimately pays for the book. The money on a $4 book would then be divided as follows:

Customer pays	$4.00
Book buyer retains 47%	1.88
Publisher collects	2.12
Publisher pays royalty of 10% on $4	.40
Money left to pay costs and profit	1.72

However, if the publisher gives the book buyer a 50 percent discount, the second paragraph then comes into force. The author's royalty is reduced to $.20 on each copy sold. Under the second paragraph the money on a $4 book would be divided as follows:

Customer pays	$4.00
Book buyer retains 50%	2.00
Publisher collects	2.00
Publisher pays royalty of 10% on $2	.20
Money left to pay costs and profit	1.80

It will be noticed that the publisher, under this modifying clause, by increasing the discount by 3 percent, gives the book buyer $.12 more on each copy sold, gives himself $.08 more on each copy sold, and reduces the author's royalty $.20 on each copy sold. Under this modifying clause it is to the publisher's advantage and profit to increase the discount.

Here is the modifying clause in the Morrow form contract:

Where the discount to wholesalers, retail distributors, book clubs, reading circles or special markets in the U.S.A. is 48%, a rate of royalty 1% lower than the prevailing rate, and with each additional 1% in discount, the royalty rate shall be further reduced by an additional one-half of 1%. In no case, however, shall the royalty be less than one-half of the prevailing rate.

Under this modifying clause a discount of 50% will divide the money as follows:

Customer pays	$4.00
Book buyer retains	2.00
Publisher collects	2.00
Publisher pays royalty of 8% on $4	.32
Money left to pay costs and profit	1.68

In other words, the publisher gives the book buyer $.12 a copy more, reducing the author's royalty by $.08 and his own collections by $.04. If enough copies are sold so that the royalty reaches the 15 percent rate, the Regnery clause becomes all the more vicious. When the normal royalty is 15 percent, the Regnery modifying clause reduces the author's royalty from $.60 to $.20, a reduction of $.40. Under the Morrow clause the author's royalty is reduced only $.08.

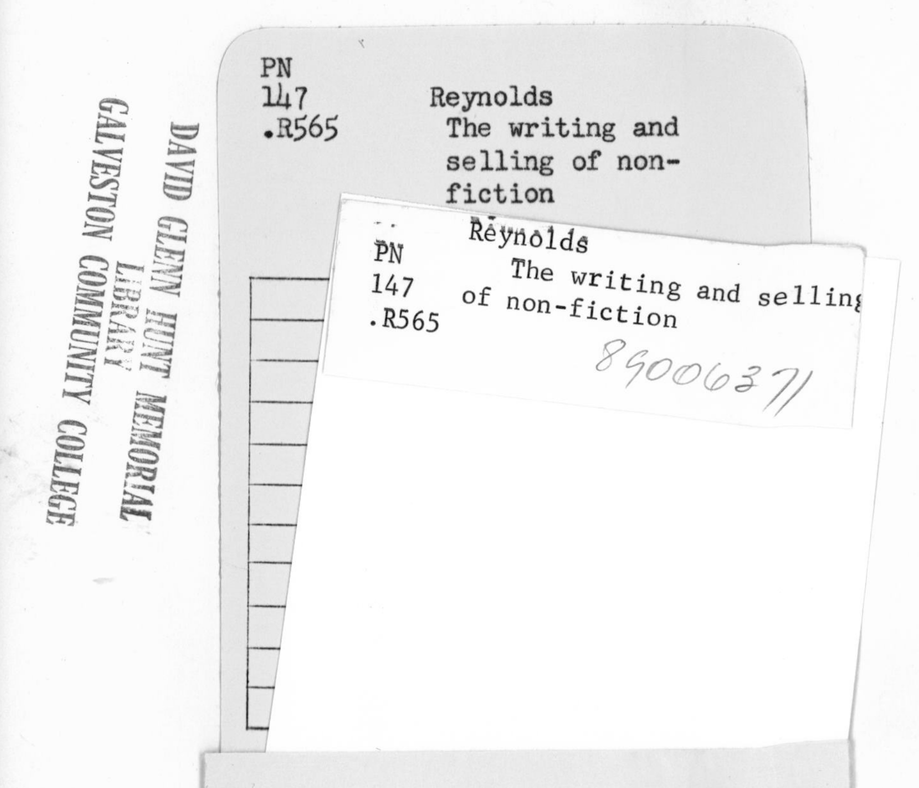

PN
147
.R565
Reynolds
The writing and
selling of non-
fiction
Reynolds
PN
147
.R565
The writing and selling
of non-fiction
89006371
DAVID GLENN HUNT MEMORIAL
LIBRARY
GALVESTON COMMUNITY COLLEGE